Endc

Sometimes our "YES," takes us t   r
make us! Again, Jenny has carried   ?
to go; in search of who we truly are
prepared for a journey that wi.   .. places waiting for
demolition, or redemption. She steps into the role as our guide leading
the way. I have had the privilege of having a front row seat in her own
journey, as her pastor and her friend. This book will set a table before
you of milk and honey; of healing, abundance, and freedom.

—Leisa Nelson
Senior Pastor, The Rock Family Worship Center
Huntsville, Alabama

Jenny Erlingsson's words are truly honey for the soul. Milk and Honey
will either make you fall in love with Jesus for the first time, or
recapture your affections for the Jesus you once knew. Wherever you
are, this book will shift the atmosphere in your heart, soul, and mind.

—Sadie Robertson
Speaker & Author of Live, Fearless & Live Original

Jenny has masterfully uncovered the solution to addressing the inner
pessimistic voice in us all. My experience in the mental health
profession has continually shown our emotional distress stems from a
flawed view of our identity; one that can only be resolved by intimacy
with God. Her ability to capture and express the inner workings of the
heart in a relaxed way, disarms our defense mechanism of wanting to
"porcupine up." This book confronts in love by holding the mirror of
God's love to our otherwise shameful selves allowing us to be
vulnerable withholding nothing.

—Viema Emmanuel-Perez, LPC
CEO & Founder of Breakthrough Holistic Services

Brilliantly written, Jenny pulls a few female characters out from scripture and expounds their story bringing depth, meaning and understanding by illuminating the life and culture of the time. From the noblest to the humblest, she shares keys each woman had that propelled them to greatness in God's eyes. By exposing her own vulnerabilities, Jenny shares personal stories of how these keys are still applicable today. Through her poetic prose and compelling questions she produces a lovely account of hope, God's redemption and faithfulness in every season of life as we as women, move towards the Father's heart and enter into the promise of "Milk and Honey."

—Lynne Chandler
Missions Pastor & Director of the Mission Intensive Training School
Bethel Church, Redding, CA

When I read Jenny's writings, I am filled with the warmth of recognizing a sister who knows Him, spends time with Him and loves Him. I am so deeply moved when someone loves Him. He loves us so much and longs for our affection and attention. I believe anyone who loves Him or wants to love Him can be drawn into deeper intimacy with their Maker by reading these beautifully transparent words of love and desire. Jenny's journey is a beautiful invitation to journey deeper into the heart of God.

—Shi-Anne Eakin
A daughter of God, Eyes on Jesus, Nashville, TN

I honor Jenny's life as she has scoured the depths of hidden things in pursuit of even greater intimacy with the One her heart loves and longs for. Jenny brings us these treasures she has found in her secret place with the Lord and has written them in this catalytic and authentic book. The stories of Jenny's life bring validation to her exhortation and encouragement to the Bride. She has gone there with the Lord—the victorious, difficult, and painful—and with all her heart calls the reader to fix forward and run after the Lover of your soul! This vision and conviction fills every page of this grand masterpiece. This book will draw you deeper into intimacy, longing, adoration, and worship for your coming Bridegroom!

—Julie King
Director of Arise, through East West Ministries International
Author of Awake and Arise, releasing April 2020

Jenny has penned another stunning book, full of life, hope and encouragement. If you find yourself in a season of wanting more or in a season of waiting for more, this book will be a lifeline for you. She has taken some of the most beautiful stories in the Bible and coupled them with her own life, taking us on a journey to find our true identity, intimacy with our Father and how to influence and empower others around us. I love everything about this book!!

—Kim Aube
Pastor, The Rock Family Worship Center, Madison
Campus

This book reaches to the heart of Identity, bringing about simple yet profound awareness of the importance of Intimacy for the ability to release Influence. Jenny takes you on an incredible journey that makes every step personal and applicable. There is richness to every page, and a beauty expressed from a heart who is living this revelation. An essential read for the daughter wanting to come into fullness as the bride of Christ.

—Suzanne Holden
Pastor, The Rock Family Worship Center Shoals Campus

I must say that Jenny has a unique ability to express the heart of God and how he values woman. Her words are comforting yet correcting, encouraging and empowering, all of it laced in His love. She is calling for the daughters to be firm and established in who we are in Him and not to discount our lives no matter how mundane or exciting. Each life has purpose in Jesus!! How wonderful to run with him to ensure it is fulfilled.

—Joy Coleman
Kingdom Sister, Madison, AL

Jenny Erlingsson has walked out the truths of the need for intimacy, holiness and consecration to the Lord as long as I have known her. I have the pleasure of knowing Jenny and her family for many years and have observed her dedication, consecration and faithfulness to the Lord and His Word from childhood. Her obedience to follow the promptings and leading of the Holy Spirit has been a witness and challenge to all.   The words of this book ring with genuineness, authenticity and coming from a deep well of His Presence because of her walk and her ability to speak to us as the Bride of Christ, His Church of these things.   Her example and faithfulness over the years is endorsement enough.

—Rita Sutton
Intercessor, The Rock Family Worship Center

Milk & Honey

In the Land

of

Fire & Ice

Cultivating Sweet Spots of Christ Centered
Identity, Intimacy, & Influence in Every Season

JENNY ERLINGSSON

Milk & Honey in the Land of Fire & Ice

Copyright © 2020 by Jenny Erlingsson

All rights reserved. This book is protected by copyright laws of the United States of America. This book may not be copied or reprinted for commercial gain or profit. The use of short quotations or occasional page copying for personal or group study is permitted and encouraged. Permission will be granted upon request.

Scripture quotations marked (NIV) are taken from the Holy Bible, New International Version®, NIV®. Copyright © 1973, 1978, 1984, 2011 by Biblica, Inc.™ Used by permission of Zondervan. All rights reserved worldwide. www.zondervan.com The "NIV" and "New International Version" are trademarks registered in the United States Patent and Trademark Office by Biblica, Inc.™ Scripture quotations marked (NLT) are taken from the Holy Bible, New Living Translation, copyright ©1996, 2004, 2015 by Tyndale House Foundation. Used by permission of Tyndale House Publishers, a Division of Tyndale House Ministries, Carol Stream, Illinois 60188. All rights reserved. Scripture quotations marked (ESV) are from the ESV® Bible (The Holy Bible, English Standard Version®), copyright © 2001 by Crossway, a publishing ministry of Good News Publishers. Used by permission. All rights reserved.

Cover & Interior Design by Jenny Erlingsson

Reach us on the Internet: www.milkandhoneywomen.com

ISBN 13 TP: 978-1-7346780-2-4

ISBN 13 HB: 978-1-7346780-4-8

ISBN 13 eBook: 978-1-7346780-3-1

ISBN 13 Large Print: 978-1-7346780-5-5

For Worldwide Distribution, Printed in the United States of America

1 2 3 4 5 6 7 8 9 10

Dedication

This book is dedicated to my 4th child Moses, whose presence in this season means more than he knows. To my mother Patience, a Jael to our family who has been loving, and prayerful and faithful to kill the enemies that have come to her door. Lastly, to my friend Tracy, who went to be with the Lord recently. She was a Deborah in the lives of so many, speaking truth in love to all who knew her.

Contents

Forward

It is always so easy to write about someone you believe in, respect and admire. I feel that way about Jenny. From the first time we met I instantly knew I wanted to be her friend. Her contagious laugh and warm personality filled every room she walked into. She is humble, incredibly kind and carries a wealth of wisdom, well beyond her years. To call her friend is a honor, but to be able to write this forward is a gift.

Whether you are familiar with Jenny or this is your first time getting aquatinted with her I can assure you that you will not be disappointed in what you are about to read. Jenny has been marked by Jesus, giving Him everything. He has captivated her and created a depth within her that we benefit from on every page of this book. When I read Jenny's first book, "Becoming His" I couldn't put it down. Each page drew me deeper into the heart of Jesus, continually causing me to discover the depth of God's love for His Daughters. "Milk and Honey" is the perfect follow up! These pages are filled with revelation, insight, and truth that is God-breathed and will touch your heart in ways where you will find yourself regularly crying as you devour this book. I know I did.

I love Jenny's ability to break down Biblical historical stories and apply them to where you and I live today. We find parts of our stories within these pages always leading us back into the arms of our Savior. Jenny has a gift to find God in the midst of our humanity, reminding us of the beautiful story He is writing through all of our lives. As you read the pages of this book you will continually be reminded of not only how loved you are by the Father but to never forget that you were created with purpose and destiny! I so believe in who Jenny is and what she carries! I believe that God is raising up a new breed of women that will display the beauty, power & love of God like never before. I believe Jenny represents this new breed and "Milk and Honey" is a part of the narrative that God is writing through His daughters. He has anointed Jenny for this time with this book.

So, I encourage you to grab a cup of coffee, or a warm cup of something, get into a quiet space and treat yourself to "Milk and Honey". Your soul will be soothed, your heart ministered to and your identity reawakened. Friends, this is more than just another book. It is nuggets of wisdom shared with us from a woman who has walked a surrendered journey with the Lord. May we not casually read these pages, but rather come expectant knowing we are going to encounter Jesus. And because of that we will never be the same.

For More Of Him,
Christa Smith
Pointblank International

Introduction

"I have come to rescue them from the hand of the Egyptians and to bring them up out of that land into a good and spacious land, a land flowing with milk and honey—"
Exodus 3:8 NIV

I had no idea what I was in for but was extremely excited. A new package had been delivered to our little home that was full of treasures for my brother and me. My mother helped open the box and we pulled out items that to some in this day and age would not seem like much. Among the contents were several VHS video tapes and a large thick book. Unbeknownst to me those items would open the door to a new life.

I often look back at those times with sweet nostalgia. I think of all that took place in the life of my mother, brother and I before more siblings were added and before my parents finally divorced. We lived in a season of struggle—my parents separated, my Nigerian mother working so hard to make ends meet. Food and housing were precious commodities. Yet in this environment the Lord birthed and established deep faith in me. He peeled back heaven and presented to me His Son. This Son I learned more of in the 1980's SuperBook video my mother ordered for me. This Son I read more about in the thick beautifully illustrated book that was my first Bible. This Jesus I saw daily in the journey my mother walked out through those hard days and years. I heard Him. I saw Him. I met Him in the midst of the toughest moments. Where fear should have otherwise ruled, His presence cast beautiful light into dark places. It was during this time that He began to woo me with the serenade that He has sung over me my entire life. He called my name. He called me daughter.

I can't tell you exactly why this has been the reoccurring theme of my life. Maybe it had to do with not always having both parents at home. The financial struggles and family issues. Of longing to please through grades, achievements, and other outward accomplishments but not feeling like that was enough. Maybe it had to do with feeling like an oddball among my classmates growing up (aren't we all though?). Always the tallest in my class. I had parents from another country so the way I talked or responded was slightly off from the rest of my peers. Whatever the reason, I now walk this thing out joyfully. Wanting to get closer, desiring to go deeper. I believe that all of us are meant to be illustrations, painting the picture of God's love in different hues. Telling His story over and over through the journey of our lives. Declaring a part of His nature that others may not be able to see. A part of His nature that He wants *us* to see too. It is God's desire for us to be His, to be positioned as His sons and daughters for now and for eternity.

I shared so much about being a daughter of God in my first book, **Becoming His: Finding Your Place as a Daughter of God.** But after releasing it I realized that I wasn't finished. The Holy Spirit did not lead me to write that book because I had figured it all out and was an expert in what it meant to be a daughter of God. Man, I was so far from it. I believe that He released it through me so that I would venture further, dig deeper and continue to position myself within Him. Everything that I thought I had already learned, everything that I essentially declared, was being tested weeks and months after the release of that message. And in the hardest and darkest moments He reminded me of what He'd already declared over me. He wanted to show me what it meant for a Father to provide for His daughter. That provision was more than I could have ever imagined. It was not about monetary value or worldly wealth. But about showing me more of His smile, of His tender mercies, of His loving discipline, of the sweetness of His embrace.

He is setting the course for not just an earthly but an eternal relationship that reaps lasting fruit and influence. He is positioning His Bride to release provision, signs and wonders and His glory upon the earth. When we come into agreement with who we are in Him, let us determine to stay there. To keep our position, to remain, to abide, to dwell in that place, which is immovable. The place no demon from hell can shift us from. We are His daughters. It's time that we live like it. That is what I want to explore more of in this journey you hold in your hands.

> **When we know who we are, we know where to go.**
> **When we know where to go, we know what to do.**
> **When we know what to do, lives are impacted with the gospel.**

Listen. I never thought I would be writing my next book in another country let alone one called the land of Fire and Ice. Y'all. I'm a Nigerian woman born and raised in the southern United States. Two degrees in Social Work and over twelve years on the pastoral staff of a large multicultural church in North Alabama. Yet here I am, surrounded by the snow covered mountains of Iceland. Volcanoes and waterfalls and lava rock just a short distance away. In a country where it is rare to see my culture and skin color and where my role is totally different from what it was just a few years ago. We moved here to be ministry workers, to do our best to join the efforts of others and further the kingdom of God. My husband was born in Iceland and I carried this nation in my womb through my four Nigerian-Icelandic mocha drops. But I never thought I would be here. I never thought the Lord would call us to come. Yet come we did. Transition came for me relentlessly. Pulling me from comfort, the familiar, from home...to plant me in a place where I could be positioned to see His glory fall. To see His Milk and Honey flow.

I will share a bit of my story throughout these pages but that is not the core of this message. It's just the personal journey that I've walked through for the last few years that I am seeing paralleled in others within the Body of Christ. This is truly a season of transition as so many have prophetically shared over the past few years. God is positioning His Bride to seek more of His presence and out of the overflow He is going to move in powerful significant ways. In this book we will take a look at what the Lord did in the lives of three specific pairs of women in the Bible and see how we can cultivate our own places of Identity, Intimacy and Influence no matter the season.

This book is broken up into three parts with five chapters in each of them. Although not necessary, the *Milk & Honey Study & Prayer Guide* can be purchased to go along with this book. You can read Milk & Honey in one sitting if you like or savor it over an extended period of time. I am well aware that many of us read multiple books at one time. I am the same, with five to seven books I am reading that I go back and forth between. I find that there are times where I need a specific insight or where God leads me to a certain book. As I pick up where I left off, the passages speak prophetically to where I am that day and moment.

I pray this book is the same for you. My hope is that there are nuggets contained within these pages that you carry with you. That there are words and phrases that trigger a deeper pursuit and deeper understanding of where you are and who God has called you to be. Mostly, I pray that you find yourself in the presence of the Lord and let Him speak directly to your heart so that you can be aligned with His heart for you. We *must* be aligned. We must be women that abide well to receive and release all that He intends for us to. **I believe there is a promise of Milk and Honey that the Lord wants to pour through you in whatever your land of Fire and Ice may be.** There are moments of encounter prepared for you. Welcome to the journey sister, you have a part in this story.

PART ONE

ESTABLISHING IDENTITY

Part One

"I will not leave you as orphans; I will come to you."
John 14:18 NIV

"Like newborn babies, crave pure spiritual milk, so that
by it you may grow up in your salvation, now that you
have tasted that the Lord is good."
1 Peter 2:2 NIV

The Vessel

The Bible says that we have these treasures hidden in jars of clay (2 Corinthians 4:7-9). We are meant to be vessels that carry the glory and power and presence of the Lord. But I find, especially when it comes to identity, many of us have cracks and chips in those vessels due to circumstances that left us broken. Because we are this way, we feel we cannot carry what we were meant to and that whatever gets poured into us flows back out. This first part of the book is dedicated to assessing our vessels to see where we are at. We'll look first at the story of the woman with the issue of blood, told in an imaginative way similar to Biblical fiction novels.

Isn't it interesting that the woman's issue was that she could not contain what was meant to remain in her, to give her life and sustenance? What are the issues that plague you and affect how you see yourself and the foundational identity of your life? You may have been a believer for many years and have operated in fullness and abundance, but over time the things you've walked through have left some cracks that you were unaware of. Or maybe the shiny veneer you were once coated in has lost its luster. Or perhaps you have been through such traumatic experiences that you don't even feel like a whole vessel any longer, just a pile of broken pieces cast on the ground. The good news is that no matter where you are or what state you are in, the Lord has something to speak to you and remind you of concerning who you are in Him. And even when you feel like you can no longer be used because of your brokenness, the Lord scoops you up in His hand, sets you up on the potter's wheel, lovingly forming you back from the beginning. Repairing those broken places into who He has always meant for you to be.

Her Moment for Identity

The Woman with the Issue of Blood
(Biblical Accounts found in Matthew 9:20-22, Mark 5:25-34, Luke 8:43-48)

I could hear the noise of a multitude outside of my modest home. This was unusual. My neighbors usually weren't that loud, especially near my house. Most tiptoed around and spoke in whispers as they passed, as if the sound of their voices would affect my condition. Or maybe they were afraid to even breath around my abode, lest the state of my body poison them like a contagious sickness. I was indeed sick. There was no doubt about that. But it was only mine to bare, only mine to carry. My loneliness told me that plainly, day after day.

I wrapped a garment around me as I peered out the window. From what I could see there was something, or maybe someone, causing a stir within the community. As I looked further, I saw a moving mass of people, growing larger by the seconds. And as the sounds of commotion carried to me, the name they called out sent a shiver up my spine.

Jesus.

Jesus! He was here again! Other times, when I was able to make out conversations or the few times I willed myself to venture out, I overheard the stories of a rabbi that brought healing wherever He went. I felt then the lingering ripple of curiosity and excitement in the air every time He came through. Twelve years ago, I would have laughed at how ridiculous it seemed. But now...now I was willing to try anything to be cured of my issue. I would do anything to free myself of the filthy rags that were my constant companion, catching a flow that never stopped. Leaking from me all my energy and strength. Seeping away the life that I should have been living. There should be more to my life than this!

A sob was at the verge of breaking through, breaking me down again. But all of a sudden, something else entirely burst in my heart and I clutched my garment to my chest, almost overcome by this new emotion. I had long forgotten hope. It was stolen away in the pockets of physicians and in the sacrifices placed on more altars than I could count. But here it was, staring me in the face, beckoning me to take a chance and go. Alluring me with a small possibility, but possibility none the less. Before I knew it, sandals were on my feet, my shawl positioned over my head and face. I was stepping outside of my home. I left my place of isolation and made my way carefully towards the crowd surrounding this Jesus. The source of my shaky hope.

The crowd moved like a river's current. People swirling around and in and out, trying to get close, trying to see. I felt their curiosity and hunger and even some anger. But all I could think of was my need and how I could get to Him. I didn't know what His usual protocol was or how one even got close enough to ask. But all I knew was that I couldn't let this chance pass me. I could not go on this way forever and maybe He could be the one to make it stop. I pushed and squeezed the best I could, covering my face, cowering low so as not to alarm anyone. I didn't need to be recognized.

I was almost out of breath, almost about to falter and then the crowd was no longer moving. Everyone stopped as an important man fell on his knees in front of the One we followed. It was as if all eternity froze in this instant and what I dreaded became a possible reality. Past disappointment threatened to topple my hope. It had taken all my energy and will just to approach, just to push past the stream of humanity, just to make it close to Jesus without being trampled. And now we were stopped. If I wasn't careful someone would notice me. They would call me out of hiding and demand that I return home. Or worse. It was a huge risk, I know.

I know.

I placed my head in my hands, catching my breath and trying to steady my shaky resolve. If I was caught the consequences would be unfathomable. I would affect everyone and place on them what had become my identifying name now. Unclean. Unclean they would whisper. Unclean they would yell. Unclean was the cry that I had to release every time I ventured out just to take in fresh air. I was a woman unclean for so long.

Twelve years ago, what should have been a normal process that came and went each month continued on abnormally. Days passed into weeks, weeks ran into months and soon gone were the years and so was everything I owned. I presented myself to the priests, made my sacrifices, prayed for healing, felt the sympathy and then disdain of my neighbors. Soon the hands that promised to help, pointed at me in blame. As if I had asked for this. As if I caused this outflow myself. With every drop of blood that spilled from my body, my own blood, my family, grew farther and farther away. At first I understood it. I was the aunt that could not hold or cherish my nieces and nephews. I could no longer embrace my mother or sisters or brothers. And the marriage that could have been arranged for me, well, that was not meant to be anymore. Each rejection dug a deeper hole in me but when my father turned away...

No. I could not think of these things anymore. I would not think of those who were meant to always love me who were no longer there. The grief threatened to drown me within its dark waters. I was a woman who could hold nothing. Life itself streamed from my womb. I wanted to kneel in the dust and never get up, but I could not let the rabbi go by without getting what I'd come for. I looked up again. The leader of the synagogue who had just approached the teacher finished His desperate request and everyone resumed their journey. The teacher was headed in the direction the man led Him. He was being led away from me.

No, I couldn't bare it. I couldn't wait a moment longer. I had heard the stories about what this Jesus could do. I had to take the chance that somehow, He could heal me too. I didn't want to make Him unclean. I would not embarrass Him in front of the crowd and have this malady laid upon Him. I remembered what I learned as a young girl and moved to my hands and knees. My energy is almost gone but I give everything I have to reach for one of the tassels at the end of His tallit. I've given everything to others to be healed and I give everything now with one reach of my arm. I will receive my healing from Him if He is who they say He is. I will agree with the authority and power that He carries and take just a little, oh just a little for myself. If not, I will die here in the dust.

My fingers grab hold of one little string from His garment and I am laid out in the ground from the effort. And as if in one accord the crowd stops again. I can barely hear a voice above the roar in my head. It is as if fire has been lit in me, licking up the blood and water and in that instant, I know. I am healed! In this pause, this pregnant moment of interruption I see everything, feel every emotion I had encountered for the past twelve years. There is so much loss, so much I wish still remained but regardless of the pain of the past, the pain of my ailment is gone. Gone! I want to laugh out loud but I need to get away as quickly as possible so no one will notice me here.

The voice speaks again and breaks through my wonder. "Who touched me?" He says. I look up long enough to see one of the men closest to Him whisper something. But Jesus puts a hand on His shoulder and shakes His head. He scans the crowd and says, "Someone touched me; I know that power has gone out from me." The tears that I had tried to keep in during this ordeal break loose and the dust mingles with the water pouring out of my eyes. I close them wishing the ground would swallow me up, but I know that I cannot go away unnoticed any longer. I was that someone, not just another person in the crowd. Not just a woman hidden away in her house, alone with her issue. I just received what I had been so desperate for all these years. This someone owed Him a response.

I made my way up with strength I did not know still existed in my body. It grew stronger and stronger until I was shaking from the power coursing through me. I got close to Him and as I looked into His tender gaze I fell at His feet. I could not stand before Him and it was not because of my former condition. The obvious love in His expression was breaking me. His look had swept over and through me. How long had it been since someone really looked at me? And how long had it been since that gaze didn't hold surface sympathy or veiled disgust? I was in the presence of power, pure beautiful loving power. And I was not worthy. But I did my best to speak, with everyone watching. I told Him, with my face to the ground, why I had touched Him and what happened to me. Before I could go on to explain myself further, I felt His hand touch my head and with another He lifted my chin until I was looking into His face. He had knelt down to get close to me. It felt like He was as close as my next breath.

"Daughter." He said, with the smile and compassion of an adoring father and brother and friend all mixed in one. "Your faith has healed you. Go in peace." The words swept over me like a cleansing rushing river. His healing in my body had been like fire but His words now were soothing to my parched and weary soul. I felt shame and fear lift from me and the hole in my heart that I never expected to be made whole was mended. Made new. In that instant I saw my memories again, but through a different filter. The filter of His love and compassion and His peace. I may have been rejected by others, but I was fully accepted by Him. He called me daughter. Daughter!

And just as quickly, He was gone. The crowd moved with Him as He continued on with the synagogue leader, a servant bringing more news. But I didn't hear the words they said. And I don't know how long I sat there in the road, in the dust, more healed and whole than I'd ever been in my entire life. The lingering sweetness of the man called Jesus sweeping around me. He had noticed me. He called me daughter.

Milk & Honey: Speak Lord

Speak Lord

The way you do so tenderly that unmasks the part of me I would
rather stay hidden.

Stay hiding instead of abiding.

Stay soaking in the ocean of rejection when you have called me
higher,

to dance on the water.

Speak Lord.

Say my name so sweetly.

Say the words you breathed from eternity.

Set straight all the thoughts I think of me with the name that
established my identity.

Speak Lord.

Lest I fall again, fail to be yours and move with the wind of doubt
and insecurity.

Bumped off course by what I think they did to me.

Off my rhythm because of my skewed perception
or even perhaps intentional rejection.

Shift my perspective.

Let me see the worlds you create with your words.

Let me see the height and breadth of your majesty that moves me
from complacency
into friendship and mystery.

Let me see the beauty you make of ashes when you speak Lord.

When you speak Lord, to fragile me.

So gently allured from insanity of striving and trying to the
safety of your shadow.

Peeking out to see your Glory overshadow, overshadowing me
with the weight of your presence.

I choose to be present in every moment.

Craving the words that you drip like honey to my lips.

The sweetness of your serenade calming my fearful heart.

You give me a new song that you and I know only,
birthed from the secret place of just you and me.

I find me fully Whole when you speak Lord
so, speak please.

Chapter One: The Sweetness of the Savior

I have been in numerous services, sessions and gatherings throughout my time knowing Christ. I have experienced Jesus among the crowd and in the hidden places of my life. There are moments when I'm swept away by worship and it's as if I could fly right out of my body. And then there are times when I cannot get low enough because of how undone the Lord has made me in His presence. It's as if His love is melting all the words and resistance in me and I am being poured out, becoming the vial of worship over His feet. In all of these times one of the most profound realizations to me is how sweet Jesus is. Many times, the words that come from my lips after a moving encounter with the Lord are, "Jesus, you are so sweet. Thank you for how sweet you are to me."

This may not seem impactful to you or like a huge revelation. The last few years we as the body of Christ have received more and more teaching on the goodness of God and I am so thankful that hearts are turning in that direction. Our God is definitely so good. He is so faithful. He is so loving. So merciful, so compassionate, so incredible. And there is a special sweetness I find in His presence that is overwhelming. He is so specific and intentional when it comes to His children.

When I am overwhelmed in those moments with Him it's because

He has pinpointed something in me that maybe I was not able to see or fathom on my own. Whether its encouragement or correction, a kiss or a kick, ha, I am always so grateful. Because like a loving Father, He presses past the surface and places attention on the inner parts of me. All because He loves me. As He loves you.

I believe this is a season where the Lord wants to intentionally lavish His love on you. He wants to woo and make whole His church, His beloved Bride. Not so that we can turn inward in what we receive but so that we are filled to overflowing and can't help but change the atmosphere wherever we go. He wants women who will saturate their surroundings with His presence, women who ooze His extravagant love to others. Women who know how to love supernaturally. Women who have tasted the sweet honey of His goodness and can't help but stir up hunger for more of Christ in themselves and those they encounter.

How will others taste and see that the Lord is good if we ourselves have not tasted of His goodness? This can't happen if we are leaky vessels. We get pummeled by situations and circumstances, by our experiences and upbringing and many times don't realize the deep damage that has been done. All we know is that in all the things that we do for relief, we can't ever seem to get beyond a temporary solution. We get filled up only to have it all seep out after the church service, the Bible Study, the time of prayer and on and on.

Was this not the case of the woman with the issue of blood? This woman who goes unnamed is mentioned in three out of the four gospels. We are not given too much of her backstory, only that she had been bleeding for twelve years. She was physically unable to function normally in society because of this issue but worse yet, she was considered unclean by Jewish law. And because of that she was to remain isolated from others. I can't imagine that life, being betrayed by your own body. The process that is supposed to be a sign of life to come, a signal that you are able to carry life as a woman, backfiring on you. Your source of posterity becomes your prison. This woman had issues upon issues, physical, spiritual, relational, and so on. She spent all her money on a cure for her disease but after twelve years even a doctor's remedy was not enough for her. Her need was too great, her disease too significant to be touched by any worldly means or methods.

We must understand that if there is a hole or wound somewhere within us, what gets poured into us will get lost within those hurts, disappointments, frustrations, pride, insecurities and failures. Those hidden wounds become cancers eating away at our inner being. This is not life in abundance. This is not the milk and honey that was promised to flow. And oh, dear one, there is so much for you to flow with. When the Lord comes, He is not just on the scene to empower you. He also has all authority and ability to bring healing to you through His resurrection power.

The healing comes not just in how much we love Jesus but in truly receiving and coming into agreement with how much He loves us. Because we love Jesus, we do for Him. But listen to this. Because Jesus loves us, He does for us. Rather He did, He does, and He will continue to do. My doing for Him is limited and nothing compared to what He has already accomplished for me. But Jesus moves with all authority, power, majesty, ability, love…do you get the picture?

Some time ago my husband and I attended a healing conference at a church in Reykjavik, the capital of Iceland (more on our Iceland journey later). A man named Chris Gore was there to teach the sessions. Chris is the director of the healing rooms at Bethel church in Redding. Instead of coming with methods and steps for healing He came with a totally different perspective than I expected. What He said has stuck with me even as I look at my own life and the circumstances that surround me at times. He said that the healing part is easy. It's the healing of our hearts, the changing of our mindsets that must happen in order for us to come into agreement with what Jesus has done for us and how He feels about us.

Nothing is too hard or impossible for Jesus to accomplish in our lives. We are so dearly loved. And it is this sweet knowledge that allows us to operate from a place of confidence and motivation. We love because He first loved us. It was because of His great love for us that He came to earth, became one of us and died in our place. We must start at this beginning for there is no other. The Father is the source of everything that we are and there is no other way to Him except through Jesus Christ. Let us take a moment and reflect on how sweet and wonderful our Jesus is. My prayer is that if you do not know Jesus at all or you don't know Him that well, His kindness will lead you to repentance and to a new beginning. Hebrews 12:2 in the NLT says:

> **"We do this by keeping our eyes on Jesus, the champion who initiates and perfects our faith. Because of the joy awaiting Him, He endured the cross, disregarding its shame. Now He is seated in the place of honor beside God's throne."**

Jesus endured the cross in obedience to the will of Father God and with you in sight. You were the joy set before Him. His desire was to see you reconciled to the Father and He found joy in the fulfillment of that relationship. Jesus came as a second Adam, the last Adam, to make right what went so terribly wrong in the garden. And in another garden, He kneeled to pray and once again submitted His will to Father God. Where the first Adam, son of God, disobeyed and ate of the tree, Jesus, a type of second Adam, the true Son of God, obeyed and placed himself on a tree of a different kind. He placed all the sins of humanity past, present and future on His shoulders, becoming the ultimate sacrifice. Jesus took on the entire wrath of God that should have been placed on us. The blood He shed trumped the blood of every spotless animal that was placed on the altar and with it our sins were washed away. When He died, the curtain of the Holy of Holies in the temple was ripped open from top to bottom. Again, God bursting out to embrace humanity, giving a way back to himself if we would choose to accept His gift. And then on the third day He rose again with resurrection power, finalizing victory over death, hell and the grave. He gave us the ability to have relationship with the Father and promised a home with Him in eternity. This is good news! This is the joy He set before himself. No wonder we can then say:

> **"For His anger lasts only a moment, but His favor lasts a lifetime! Weeping may last through the night, but joy comes with the morning." Psalm 30:5 NLT**

> **"Don't you see how wonderfully kind, tolerant, and patient God is with you? Does this mean nothing to you? Can't you see that His kindness is intended to turn you from your sin?" Romans 2:4 NLT**

So, considering all that Jesus has done for us, what excuse do we have to not be made free? He is so sweet, so exceedingly kind. He pours His love on you in order for you to come close. His desire is for all of us to turn from the sin and the ways that lead to death and come into agreement with the life abundant He offers us. Not a life measured solely by earthly success, but by agreeing with heaven and being the earth that heaven kisses. An abundant life is a life flowing with the goodness of God, overflowing out of relationship with Him.

> **"If we confess our sins, He is faithful and just and will forgive us our sins and purify us from all unrighteousness." 1 John 1:9 NLT**

It is so simple. Our part to play is so small in comparison to what Jesus gives us in exchange. He simply asks for us to confess our sins, to be out and open with the things that keep us from experiencing the life He offers. He willingly takes our burdens and instead offers us His faithfulness, His justice, His forgiveness and purification. He gives what we never would have been able to give ourselves. It reminds me of one of my favorite verses in **Jeremiah 33:3 "Call to me and I will tell you great and unsearchable things you know not of."** In the same way He says confess, cry out, call out to me in repentance and I am faithful to do so much more than you can even imagine. It's as simple as the words on your very next breath. He already paid the price to make it so.

"See how very much our Father loves us, for He calls us His children, and that is what we are!"
1 John 3:1a NLT

When we choose to be chosen, confess our sins and receive the gift of salvation offered to us by Jesus, we are now co-heirs with Christ. We are born into a new kingdom and given an eternal family. We forever belong not to something but to someone, to the Father. He calls us His children, breaking us from every lie, accusation and belief that tells us that we don't belong. The kingdom is about family. You have a part to play and a Father to lean on. He will never leave you nor forsake you. When He looks at you, He sees the sacrifice of His son and the beautiful bride His son is coming back for. We are a church beautified and empowered by the Holy Spirit, the gift and deposit Jesus released to us as He returned to the Father. A promise of what was to come and the source of abundant life.

"So, you have not received a spirit that makes you fearful slaves. Instead, you received God's Spirit when He adopted you as His own children. Now we call Him, "Abba, Father." Romans 8:15 NLT

My dear sister, do you understand the gift we have been given? May joy stir up inside of you. May peace settle your fear and guard your heart and mind. You have a Father that not only loves you, sent His son to pay the price for you, invited you into relationship with Him and filled you with His Holy Spirit…but He also enjoys you, yes YOU! The Lord takes great delight in you. He is a Father that enjoys spending time with His children and partnering with them to see His kingdom come upon this earth. He delights in you may you enjoy Him also.

"For the LORD your God is living among you. He is a mighty savior. He will take delight in you with

gladness. With His love, He will calm all your fears. He will rejoice over you with joyful songs." Zephaniah 3:17 NLT

"Delight yourself in the Lord and He will give you the desires of your heart" Psalm 37:4 ESV

We are invited to enter into the sweetest love this world has ever known. We have access to the heart of God if we would choose to position ourselves and go deeper and further in, throwing off the things that keep us away from His presence. He does not give us anything that we are unable to carry. Rather we are able to throw our burdens to Him and He gives us a weight that is fit to us, that is made specifically for our lives to hold.

"Give all your worries and cares to God, for He cares about you." 1 Peter 5:7 NLT

"All praise to God, the Father of our Lord Jesus Christ, who has blessed us with every spiritual blessing in the heavenly realms because we are united with Christ. Even before He made the world, God loved us and chose us in Christ to be holy and without fault in His eyes. God decided in advance to adopt us into His own family by bringing us to himself through Jesus Christ. This is what He wanted to do, and it gave Him great pleasure. So we praise God for the glorious grace He has poured out on us who belong to His dear Son. He is so rich in kindness and grace that He purchased our freedom with the blood of His Son and forgave our sins. He has showered His kindness on us, along with all wisdom and understanding." Ephesians 1:3-8 NLT

Doesn't this cause worship to stir in your heart? There are truly no words adequate to describe what we have because of what Jesus did for us. He was slain before the earth was formed. The Lord already had a solution for our sin in place before we made the first decision to sin. He made a way for our healing and deliverance before we even needed it. Our Lord is faithful, loving and so thorough. He loves us patiently and compassionately, leaving no stone unturned throughout our lives as we submit ourselves to His pruning and care. Everything that Jesus did was what the Father was doing.

He showed us that we have a Father that is not far off or distant, but who longs for us to be close to Him. This is the One who has called you to not just survive in life, barely making it from one day to the next. He has destined you to live your life in abundance. He has supernatural provision that He is flowing to you and through you to affect those around you. It's the sweetness of His presence, His overwhelming love and glory that we get to house and release.

Take a moment even now to respond to Him in worship. It's not just about a song or a sound, it is as simple as fixing your eyes on Jesus as Hebrews 12:2 says. Ask Him to show you a glimpse of His beautiful face, of His ways. And if you don't know Him, read over the verses I placed here again, confess your sin, turn away from the things that separated you, receive His free gift of salvation and ask Him to be Lord, the absolute ruler of your life.

Let us cover this journey together in adoration and praise towards the one who is more than worthy of it. Let's shift the atmosphere in our homes even now as we prepare to dive further into this book.

Jesus. How worthy you are. There is truly no one like you and no one compares to you. Thank you for enduring the cross for us. For considering it joy to see us joined to the Father. So much so that you gave up everything and carried all of our sins to pay the ultimate price for our freedom. And in the same moment you brought about our salvation, you made a way for our healing. You bore wounds on your back in order for us not to bear wounds in our body and mind. You did a complete work on the cross in order for us to be complete people. Words are not enough to tell our gratitude. As we go further into this book, we ask that you go with us. Would you cover every revelation, every step and every process? We want to walk this out with you. And we are thankful for the alignment that will come in this journey, equipping us to overflow with your milk and honey in our land of promise. In Jesus name, Amen.

Chapter Two: Healing is on the Way

The Bible is full of extraordinary testimonies. Stories that make us stand back and wonder at the raw truth, the grim reality, and the beauty that comes out of impossibilities. It is Jesus himself, wrapped up in eternal words as He was wrapped up in human flesh. Making a way for relationship that we could never attain to in and of ourselves. Ever pressing, ever seeking, ever working on the inside of us as we ponder His words and ingest them as part of our daily diet. These words made up of the testimony of multitudes of people written by numerous writers. Their pens guided by the authority and anointing of the Holy Spirit. In the Bible we behold the narrative of the ages written down by the Narrator himself, the one who had a front row seat to every act of creation.

When I read the Word of God, I see so many accounts of men and women that are heartbreaking and amazing. And there are some that continue to leave me pondering and hungry for more because of the sweet mystery wrapped up within the history that is presented. The story of the woman with the issue of blood and the dying daughter of Jairus is one of those stories. At the beginning of Part 1, I attempted to give you a glimpse into my imaginative interpretation of that particular woman's encounter with Jesus. But we truly don't know what her back story was and what her thoughts were besides what the writers of

Matthew, Mark and Luke detail for us. She determined that if she could only touch the hem of Jesus' garment, she would receive her healing. But little did she know she was placed in the middle of more. Some would say it was a cosmic coincidence, but I know that it was a divinely orchestrated appointment. In the Lord's design, He crossed the paths of two women to show them His special care and attention.

I had a situation that happened a few years ago where two women who I love dearly spoke words over my life that crossed paths in the most prophetic and specific ways. They gave me these words separately which heightened the confirmation that the Lord was highlighting something that was important for me to grasp. I was being set up for breakthrough. The first word came when we were finishing up a late morning women's gathering. I had invited this first woman to share with the ladies and at the end we stood around talking. After a few minutes she directed her attention to me and said, "Jenny, I have something from the Lord for you."

I don't know about you but in those moments two things happen to me simultaneously. A shiver of excitement runs through me as I think of the Lord stopping someone else to speak something just for me. How sweet is that of Him. But also, a slight dread comes because whether the word is encouragement or warning, there is a choice that will have to be made. And usually it's one of discomfort. Anyone else with me? I mean, you can't grab a hold of something new by staying where you are, holding on to everything else you've been comfortable with. The Lord is always extending His hand to us, to agree with His heart over our lives. But man…so many times we don't want to let go of whatever it is that is bringing satisfaction to us, no matter how temporary.

So, with parallel thoughts running but with the bravery of well-experienced Pentecostal girl I told her to lay it on me. She is a trusted intercessor and walks in deep intimacy with the Lord, so I knew that she wasn't playing with what she was about to share. I won't go into detail with the fullness of the word, but she told me that she felt like the Lord was saying that I needed to change my wineskins. That I was operating with old wineskins and that I needed to replace them with new ones. I needed wineskins that would be able to stretch and grow. Because God was bringing something new, a new anointing. But if I didn't change out my wineskins, what He wanted to pour out would spill on the ground. Wow! It was a word that fit right between the two streams of thought that I had. I was both encouraged and contemplating what it meant for me. God was bringing something new and powerful into my life, BUT, if I didn't step into this change, I could miss it. The problem was I wasn't sure what it was or exactly what I needed to do.

A few days later, another friend texted me that she'd had a dream about me that she wanted to share. I've known this friend for years and she has always been good at giving me Spirit-filled practical advice, correction and encouragement. I trusted that what she had to share was going to be something I needed. She told me that in the dream I was wearing old clothing. She knew specifically that they were old because they were *her* clothes. If you know her, you would know that any article of clothing that she owns would barely fit me. Our differences in height are significant. I call her my "fun size candy bar" friend and me the "King size bar." She felt like the Lord was using that dream to speak something to me about old ways, old habits, old seasons. As soon as she told me the dream, I knew that this was connected to the word about old wineskins that I had just received. I took a few days to ponder and pray about what this could mean for me because I knew that God needed to bring some change into my life in order to deliver me from whatever the old wineskin/old garments were. But I wasn't quite sure what it was. All I knew was that I didn't want the good new thing He was bringing in my life to be wasted.

After a few days I decided to look up what the Bible said about old wineskins and old garments. My hope was to study several verses and allow the Holy Spirit to shine a light on what I needed to do. What I found was more than I expected. Not only did I find old wineskins and old garments listed in a passage together in Matthew chapter nine, but it led up to the healing of the woman with the issue and Jairus' daughter. Jesus is teaching His disciples about wineskins and garments when He is literally interrupted by Jairus coming to share about His daughter. Here is what the passage says in the NIV translation:

> **"No one sews a patch of unshrunk cloth on an old garment, for the patch will pull away from the garment, making the tear worse. Neither do people pour new wine into old wineskins. If they do, the skins will burst; the wine will run out and the wineskins will be ruined. No, they pour new wine into new wineskins, and both are preserved." While He was saying this, a synagogue leader came and knelt before Him and said, "My daughter has just died. But come and put your hand on her, and she will live." Matthew 9:16-18 NIV**

In that moment, I still didn't know the specifics of what I needed to let go of. I will speak more of the unfolding of these words in later chapters. But I knew that as I submitted myself to the Lord, He would begin to unwrap the old from my life. And I knew that the story of the women was a promise. He was going to pour out an anointing and new mantle on my life that affected women especially. How could my friends have known that in their obedience to share prophetically with me, that they would be sharing within days of one another. And that they would be sharing one half of a whole message that the Lord was speaking to me about my present and my future? Jesus' movements are so purposed and intentional. And it was the same for the two women that are currently in our focus.

Let's take a look at the actual Biblical account of the woman with the issue and the daughter of Jairus. Even though Matthew 9 is the one that spoke so prophetically to me after those words, the one I will pull from here is the account found in Mark 5:21-42. As you read ask the Holy Spirit to open your heart and give *you* eyes to see. There are seeds He is planting as we journey through this together that will come to fruition in these moments as well as in moments to come.

"When Jesus had again crossed over by boat to the other side of the lake, a large crowd gathered around Him while He was by the lake. Then one of the synagogue leaders, named Jairus, came, and when He saw Jesus, He fell at His feet. He pleaded earnestly with Him, "My little daughter is dying. Please come and put your hands on her so that she will be healed and live." So Jesus went with Him. A large crowd followed and pressed around Him. And a woman was there who had been subject to bleeding for twelve years. She had suffered a great deal under the care of many doctors and had spent all she had, yet instead of getting better she grew worse. When she heard about Jesus, she came up behind Him in the crowd and touched His cloak, because she thought, "If I just touch His clothes, I will be healed." Immediately her bleeding stopped and she felt in her body that she was freed from her suffering. At once Jesus realized that power had gone out from Him. He turned around in the crowd and asked, "Who touched my clothes?" "You see the people crowding against you," His disciples answered, "and yet you can ask, 'Who touched me?'" But Jesus kept looking around to see who had done it. Then the woman, knowing what had happened to her, came and fell at His feet and, trembling with fear, told Him the whole truth. He said to her, "Daughter, your faith has healed you. Go in peace and be freed from your suffering." While Jesus was still speaking, some people came from the house of Jairus, the synagogue leader. "Your daughter is dead," they said. "Why bother the teacher anymore?" Overhearing what they said, Jesus told Him, "Don't be afraid; just believe." He did not let anyone follow Him except Peter, James and John the brother of James. When they came to the home of the synagogue leader, Jesus saw a commotion, with people crying and wailing loudly. He went in and said to them, "Why all this commotion and wailing? The child is not dead but asleep." But they laughed at Him. After He put them all out, He took the child's father and mother and the disciples who were with Him, and went in where the child was. He took her by the hand and said to her, "Talitha koum!" (which means "Little girl, I say to you, get up!"). Immediately the girl stood up and began to walk around (she was twelve years old). At this they were completely astonished." Mark 5:21-42 NIV**

There is so much in this story to unpack. I do not want to do a Bible exposition for you in this moment but would rather paint a picture. A beautiful portrait of our Lord and the women that that He brought significant life change to.

Imagine the woman and a condition that started twelve years before her encounter with Jesus. She is bone weary tired and has lost all provision. What she needed to sustain herself has been lost to doctors in order to find a cure. We can only assume she wasn't around family and was isolated because of her condition. In those times she would have been considered unclean, like every other woman was during their monthly period. Yet for twelve years there was never a moment that she could remove the label of unclean from her life. The bleeding was constant and so was her loss.

About the same time her bleeding started, somewhere another woman was releasing blood and water as she gave birth to a beautiful baby girl. This girl was cleaned and rubbed with salt and placed on her mother's chest. She was blessed by her father and was obviously cherished by both of her parents. As the daughter of the synagogue leader she grew up in a prominent family and was a part of a thriving community. She got to be a part of what the woman with the issue of blood was now shunned from. Yet from some unknown cause, this little girl became sick and was dying. Who knows how long her father waited? Who knows how much money he himself spent on doctors to help his daughter. But whatever he and his wife did, their daughter was dying and there was no one else to help her.

12 years. Two daughters. Two points of desperation.

In our logical minds, it seems to make more sense for Jesus to tend to the needs of Jairus first. Especially since the woman with the issue did in fact receive her healing when she touched Him. Jesus didn't have to do or say anything else. She got what she came for, but Jesus wanted to give her so much more. Jesus was on His way to Jairus's house in response to his request, yet He paused for the one. Isn't that Jesus' way all throughout scripture? He leaves the 99 for the one. Not that the majority is not important or valued. But He wants the "one" to know that she or he is never lost in the crowd. And this illustrates to others within the "99" that if they were to ever fall or struggle or be left behind, Jesus will never leave them in favor of the majority. He values us all individually and loves us with unswerving devotion.

To be honest, there have been times in my life where that is hard for me to grasp. For whatever reason I have been gifted/burdened with an overwhelming sense of justice and fairness. It has served me and others well in some instances and at other times, well, maybe it brought more complication into a situation than I intended. God is a God of true justice, but His ways are not boxed in by our opinions or perspectives. Just because something seems right or fair in our eyes doesn't mean it's the most complete plan in the eyes of the Lord.

And in this instance the better way for Jesus was to pause and bring complete healing to another daughter before He even approached the daughter of Jairus. This wasn't a lack of compassion on the part of Jesus towards the child. This situation wasn't an emergency for Him because He was fully confident in His ability to bring healing and ultimately resurrection to this beloved girl. We may not understand those ways, especially when it comes to our situations and especially when we have suffered loss. But no unexpected outcome takes away from Jesus' ability, compassion and power.

In the story of these two women, healing power flowed and moved around Jesus with such potency that the woman with the issue couldn't help but get totally changed. She was changed just from grabbing a hold of a tassel that hung from His outer garment, from His prayer shawl. This tassel is called the *tzitzit*[1] in Hebrew. They hung on the corners of the prayer shawls or tallit that were worn in those times. These were intended to remind the wearer of the commandments, the Word of God. They also represented the authority of the wearer and so in this case, the authority of Jesus.[2] This woman grabbed a hold of God's word for her life and believed in the authority and ability of Jesus to carry out her healing.

This story echoes another one about a woman and her redeemer that is found in the Old Testament. Ruth did something similar at the direction of her mother-in-law. In order to save the family line of her deceased husband, Ruth went to Boaz, a distant relative, uncovered his feet and lay there. When he awoke, she told him that he was her kinsman redeemer and to spread the corner of his garment over her. She was grabbing a hold of his ability to redeem her family and coming into agreement with the commandments and authority that the edges of his garment represented. You can read more about this in the book of Ruth chapter 3. Ruth positioned herself in the way of redemption when she decided that she would follow Naomi's God and serve Him as her own. And that simple but courageous choice set her up for more than she could have imagined.

Healing is coming. Healing is on the way, heading your direction. But on that way, on that path, who else does Jesus want to encounter? Our deliverance and destiny are not just for us alone. I promise you, if you were the only one, the Lord would stop for you. His compassion is never spread thin, it is concentrated and complete and unconditional for every one of His children. But the beauty in the kingdom is that we are a body. We affect others in the body of Christ. And beyond that we also have ability to affect and influence those who do not know Christ. We can set things in motion by our obedience and faithfulness. And in another beautiful and mysterious way, we can facilitate much shift in the atmosphere from our brokenness and our cries of help to our Savior.

The despair and grief of Jairus caused him to cry out for help. He was a synagogue leader who was so desperate for his daughter to be healed that instead of sending a servant or anyone else in his place, he ran to Jesus and fell at His feet. He begged the Savior to come and heal his daughter who we discover is at death's door. After just a few minutes of delay, because another daughter needed to be healed, Jairus finds out that his precious daughter has died.

In that moment, I can imagine that all hope was lost for him. You know how it is for us. In a blink of an eye, our circumstance can change and regret, despair, denial, blame, and grief roll into one ball of shock. Maybe if he had gone to Jesus sooner it would not have turned out this way. Or maybe if the woman had not approached. Or maybe if Jesus had not been so concerned about having her show herself.

But Jesus' plan for Jairus' daughter was more than what her parents could have imagined. This little girl born around the same time this woman's bleeding started would be used in a powerful way to facilitate healing to a woman who thought she would never be free. Her circumstances positioned another woman for her breakthrough. Resurrection was on the path that day. Resurrection power was on His way to a dead girl. And when another woman crossed paths, just a little morsel, just a little touch of His garment was more than enough to bring life to her body.

Don't misunderstand this. This girl was not born to be sacrificed for this woman's healing. But just like Abraham and Isaac, what a beautiful foreshadowing of what Jesus would ultimately do for all people. He was born to be with us, mingle with us, and on the way to the cross brought healing and deliverance and hope wherever He went. There was healing on the way before the cross and after the cross healing finds its way to others through the blood Jesus shed. Through His finished work. Through born again, redeemed and healed people who operate with the resurrection power (Romans 6:10-11) that dwells in them through Holy Spirit. You may even feel like you are in a dark moment. A place where you are struggling to remember who you are and feel as if you can't even speak life into where you are even right now. But as you cry out to Jesus and even as others cry out on your behalf, I have to wonder…who is being positioned for breakthrough because Jesus is on His way to you? What deliverance is waiting for you as you place yourself on the way?

We do not need to give up as we cry out for breakthrough from where we are and for whatever situation it is for. Jesus is on the way and only eternity will tell what moves He makes in the lives of others as He makes His way to you. Beloved Daughter, your cry of brokenness and need does not disqualify you from bringing impact. On the contrary, as you reach for Him you draw Him in like a magnet. The Bible says in James 4:8 that when we draw near to God, He will draw near to us. Read it for yourself and let the implications sink deep into your heart.

> **"Come near to God and He will come near to you. Wash your hands, you sinners, and purify your hearts, you double-minded. Grieve, mourn and wail. Change your laughter to mourning and your joy to gloom. Humble yourselves before the Lord, and He will lift you up." James 4:8-10 NIV**

I need you to understand the beauty of our Savior and the word of God. He does not want you to remain as you are, so He encourages you to not remain *where* you are. He beckons you to come and be cleansed of any sin, any thought process, any habit or addiction or even view of yourself that keeps you from drawing near. He wants you to be honest with that process, to grieve, to mourn, to wail, to not hold back, to not keep silent. Your bold broken crying out puts you in a place of humility. Like a father grasping for a single hope, calling for one man to heal His beloved daughter. Like a woman, laying herself in the dirt, at risk of being trampled by the crowd, grasping for a single thread of Jesus' cloak. And in the process, being reminded that she was still a daughter.

> ## Establish
>
> 1. Are there any issues in your life that you've allowed to define your identity?
>
> 2. If you have not done so already, take some time today and vocally express your need, your issue, your heart's cry to the Father. Maybe your struggle is not necessarily an issue but a dream you have. Vocalize your heart to the Lord and watch as He makes His way to you.

Milk & Honey: It is Me

It is me.

Dust mingling with tears as they throw me to your feet.

They have caught me.

Caught up in the counterfeits I thought I needed to feed me, to feel me.

I succumbed to lies,

using what is temporary and broken to soothe within me what was hurting.

In transition and change,

grasping for chains to hold on to but instead have held me bound.

They led me there and now have thrown me down.

Cast me to you for judgement and accusation.

Surrounded by a jury of me.

I see now.

I see through the mud more clearly than I did before.

It is me.

Prostituting my emotions and time and energy.

Giving myself to forget this pain of separation and loss.

Raw and uncovered, so then triggered

and under more pressure than was ever mine to take.

So here I am, my life in your hand yet

your hands instead reach down to the dirt where I lay.

Writing, speaking serenade of creation, you impress new words into my soul.

Of beauty and breaking and you break my expectations into pieces.

Then you speak,

with the peace and fire of the Father and stones drop as they falter

and my old accusations shrink back into the shadows.

You lift my head, compassion and strength in your gaze.

You see me where I am and love me the same.

You free me from the idolatry and adultery of my heart.

Giving me a new path to walk...with you.

Your intention from the start.

Chapter Three: Loose the Lies

Let's rip off the band-aid, shall we? Talk about crying out. Let's stop covering the areas of our pain and weakness, our heavy weights and hindrances with temporary fixes that have no ability to last. I know it's painful. Those areas may have been our source of comfort but let's not fool ourselves into thinking our ignorance will always be bliss. We must begin like this if we are to ever really move forward. We must get to the source of the lies we believe, the hiccups and hang ups that halt the full power of our voice.

Are you still here? On that pathway in your heart, ready to be repositioned but maybe don't have the ability to move your feet? Many times, we try the temporary fixes unaware or too caught up to care that tangled tripping roots lay about us. Halting our steps, keeping us from moving to wide open spaces of fresh air and possibilities. Now don't get me wrong. The intention is for us to release a beautiful fragrance into places that need the purification of the Holy Spirit. But for now, we must assess where we are and what our source is. What you take in must originate from the Holy Spirit. Then you can overflow with what you need to release. Let's do a little preliminary work. Let's be honest with ourselves and where we stand.

Those roots at your feet, keeping you bound, holding you back, must be uprooted. Cords cut off. Chains broken. What are some reasons why we stay where we are and therefore think that our voice is silenced?

- ○ **Shame- I can't believe what I did.**

- ○ **Fear – If I do, what will happen?**

- ○ **Insecurity – I am not good enough.**

These are the voices that speak to us. The seeds that get planted in our hearts by circumstances and get hammered in by the lies of the enemy. If they are not dug up quickly, they grow and get deeper, forming root systems in our lives. Those begin to affect the ground we stand on, making the way bumpy, keeping us held down and chained to a circumstance that we need to break free from.

You see why a simple band aid does not suffice to bring us to the place of healing that we need to be. There are roots that are intent on choking the life out of you, squeezing your chest, stealing your breath and silencing you from even making a sound. I'm not even speaking of your call yet, of how you can influence people. I'm talking about you and your ability to cry out, to cry out for your own deliverance if needed. To be honest about your pain and make your way to breakthrough.

One of the saddest moments in the Bible to me is when Tamar, the daughter of King David was raped by her half-brother Amnom. For those of you that have walked through similar situations I cannot imagine the horror and injustice of what you went through. Her innocence was brutally taken from her and then she proceeded to cry out in her grief. This next part is what makes this story such a tragic one. She went to her brother and was told to stay silent. He probably thought he was sincerely bringing comfort by telling her to remain calm. But instead he halted Tamar's ability to release her emotion and trauma, which would have allowed her to move forward on a journey towards healing. And the Bible says in 2nd Samuel 13:20 that she "lived in her brother Absalom's house, a desolate woman." That desolation wasn't intended to be her identification. Every step in this horrible experience added another layer to Tamar, from the abuse, to the inaction of her father, to the silencing from her brother. These circumstances caused a lie to take root in her life that was never supposed to be there.

Many times, we have been fooled into believing that silence is our salvation, that not saying anything is our healing. We put on the band-aid, shut our mouths and hope time will relieve what holds us. But these temporary covers are not sufficient. And all the while our roots affect relationships, hinder our finances, halt our freedom. Listen. I'm a firm believer that Jesus accomplished all things at the cross. When He said it is finished, it was done. Period. But I wonder how many things we allow to be planted in our heart after the fact. What do we hold on to in fear when we don't want to step out in faith? When we don't want to forgive, like Jesus has forgiven us. If we are not operating in fullness, regardless of the season, we need to ask Holy Spirit to reveal what is holding us back. Trusting that if He shows us something, large or small, He has made a way to be free from it.

The lie for the woman who touched Jesus' garment was that she was hidden and unnoticed, only identified by her disease. The lie for Jairus was that his daughter was beyond hope and no longer a candidate for a miracle. There came a moment that the woman had to break agreement with the sickness that defined her for so long and then come into agreement with what Jesus did for her. Her identity was not intended to be "the woman with the issue of blood" as we call her. Unclean was not supposed to be her name and therefore who she was. Her condition and place in society was real, it was fact. But the lie was that those things defined her or undermined her worth. She had to let go of the deception that kept her boxed into her house and step past her threshold. She had to make a move to get a hold of the healing she was longing for. Her actions silenced the voice of every doctor, every failed procedure, every financial limitation. She decided to believe that there was still a chance for her to be free.

In the same way, when Jesus made it to the house of Jairus to heal His dead daughter, He removed every person from the room except for three of His disciples and the girl's parents. He would not let lies and unbelief linger near the place He was trying to bring life to. His reality was so different than the circumstance before Him. The little girl was dead but to Jesus, she was only sleeping. It just took a simple word from Him to "wake her up". Think about that. The truth of the unseen is bigger than your circumstance. When we decide to break off the lies that we have believed about ourselves and others, we tap into heaven's perspective and see with eyes of possibility. This is the type of environment that miracles take place in. These are the times when we can encounter the supernatural love and provision of our heavenly Father.

I had one such encounter at a friend's house several years ago that left me undone, freeing me from the lies that I believed over myself and my family. It was the place where I saw the old garments and old wine skins begin to unravel from my life. We were in a moment of worship after good food and conversation. As the guitar played and another friend sang over the room, I closed my eyes and saw an image of a lion approaching me. As He came closer, I could feel His strength, power and absolute love. Soon, He was so close that the image of His face filled my mind's eye. I couldn't see anything else but Him. He looked at me with a fiery gaze and began to roar. Even now, my heart swells as I think about that night and the sound of the Lord's roar in my ear. Then I heard Him say that He was roaring away all the lies that I had believed for so long. He was silencing the voices that I was listening to over His own and roaring His truth into my ears. I was *beloved*. I was *protected*. I was *cared for*. He reminded me that he was safe and so good.

You see, several years before this we had some deaths take place within a few months of each other that affected close friends of mine. We prayed and interceded and believed and hoped for a miracle for one. The other death came out of nowhere, so we were left reeling in shock. I remember sitting in a service one day and seeing a picture of a lion in the middle of a valley. And in my heart, I told the Lord that I believed that He was good, but I didn't know if He was safe, echoing the words of the Lucy from C.S. Lewis' Narnia series. I knew that He had all power to heal and to protect but I was having a hard time grasping the reason why He didn't come through in the way we needed Him to in these situations. So, I saw myself backing up from that lion, remaining far enough away to not get hurt by the mysteries I could not answer.

Now back to that moment in worship. Oh, how sweet our Jesus is. How loving and tender and merciful. Taking in our fragility and limitations as humans and making a way for us over and over again. So, in this encounter as I drew near in worship, Jesus stepped towards me. He got so close so that all I could see was Him. And He didn't just speak truth over me. He *is* Truth. I saw Him grow bigger and bigger until this lion was the size of a large wall or building. And then I saw myself lie down next to Him, curled up and tucked into His side. He followed up his words and showed me that He was good and safe, even if His definition was different from mine. He reminded me that He was my cover and I could trust Him.

That night I broke free of the lies that I had believed about the Lord and in turn was believing about myself and others. And that breakthrough went a step further later on in the night, which I will speak to in a later chapter. He roared everything away that had been haunting my thoughts and settling into my mindset and even behavior. This allowed me to continue to move forward into the new season He was preparing for my family. I was not to go about quietly within my insecurity and shame and fear any longer. And neither are you. My sister it is time to uproot what is trying to take hold of you. Time to cut off what is keeping you back. Time to silence the voice that would cause you to stay hidden in desolation. You may be in a hidden season but it's not His desire for you to remain desolate. Hope is not lost. No not all. On the contrary, our Hope has found His way to you and He calls you, dear one, by name.

Establish

1. What lies have you believed over various different situations in your life? Or, what accusations from the enemy have you allowed yourself to come into agreement with? Take time to repent for what you have believed and let the Lord minister to your heart as you remove the darts from the enemy.

2. Now, ask the Lord what truth He wants to put in place of those lies or accusations. Write them down. If you are having trouble hearing His voice, open your Bible and let Him speak to you. Underline or write down the words that set your heart on fire, burning away impurities, marking you with His love.

Chapter Four: Healed and Whole

Remember again the woman with the issue. He brought healing to her body, ridding her of her infirmity. But then He filled her back up again with words that would lead to her life overflowing. He called her daughter and gave her what she needed to fill the desolate and lonely places in her life. Or remember the daughter He brought back to life. He called her out, removed the spirit of death over her and told her parents to give her something to eat. Jesus doesn't just meet one need when He encounters people. He always seems to go past the surface, giving more than we came for, impacting in a whole and holistic way.

I first learned about the word "holistic" when I was in college studying social work. When many hear that term, they think it has to do primarily with alternative medicines and food. That is a part of the holistic movement but not the entirety of the definition. Holistic care or holism essentially means "care of the entire patient in all aspects of well-being, including physical, psychological, and social."[1] When it is used in relation to a specific field like psychology or medicine it is about treating an individual in consideration of more factors and variables. In Social work, a person is viewed not just for the issue they need case management or intervention for, but in light of the systems that they are a part of in their everyday life. Family, environmental, social, financial, medical history, age, culture and so on. As I heard it over and over throughout the years, I realized how necessary this term was within the Body of Christ. It gave this often self-righteous, prideful and strong willed follower of Jesus more compassion and patience with people. It was a humbling experience and invaluable asset as I started working full time on the pastoral staff of my church in Huntsville, Alabama.

Think about how many times you have been judged based on a snapshot of your life. Boxed in as a result of just a few incidents or someone's limited perspective of you. It stinks and it's not fair and that unfortunately is the culture we live in. I don't know about you but I strongly dislike being misrepresented. It bothers me even when I know I haven't been transparent enough to give someone an in-depth look into who I really am. Because maybe the very situations that allow others to see who we really are, are the very things that cause us to keep the walls up.

So, the cycle of unfounded judgement and criticism continues, and we walk around imprisoned by the residual of what we used to walk in. This is where the beauty of a holistic perspective shines through. When you have this perspective with the anointing of the Holy Spirit you can be a force for real change and transformation in someone's life, not to mention your own. It will allow you to ask the hard, truthful questions that go beyond the surface and into deeper issues. It will position you, as you operate in true love and compassion, to pull down prophetic insight from heaven, seeing with the eyes of Jesus. As you are positioned in that place you will find that this same holism extends to you too. You will be able to give yourself grace and learn how to be patient with the you that is still becoming like Christ.

This is a crucial mindset to have not only for healing to take place but so that we will see people and ourselves made whole. Just the word itself is like a deep breath, expanding the lungs, filling every place that has been left behind, hidden in shadows. Jesus is not interested in partial work. He sees holistically, if you will, taking into account everything we have been through and shining light on those dark places we thought no one noticed. He goes deep with us, revealing the places that need to come up and bringing wholeness to the areas of our brokenness.

We see this all throughout the ministry of Jesus. Especially with the women He encountered. He always brought what they needed and then gave opportunity for them to go deeper. He didn't waste time and He didn't stay in the shallow end of the pool. The Samaritan woman thought she was in a discussion about water and then Jesus pulls the husband card, lays out her business, and ultimately leads her into a discussion on worship. The woman caught in adultery thought her life was over but not only did Jesus flip the script on her accusers, He also empowered her to leave that place with a clean slate, encouraging her to leave behind her sin. Jesus didn't just deal with the symptoms of Mary Magdalene's affliction; He drove the demons out that were tormenting her and gave her a place to belong among his followers.

We see this even more clearly and tenderly in Jesus' encounter with the woman with the issue of blood. She had faith to believe that she would be healed and so she reached out and touched the edge of Jesus' garment. The story could have ended there with Jesus continuing on His way to Jairus' daughter and the woman receiving what she came for. But Jesus always gives you more than what you came for. When the Bible talks about an abundant life it's not just about finances and provision. It's about being whole— body, mind, soul and spirit. When Jesus encountered this woman, He saw past what she presented. She was a wounded, lonely woman and Jesus wanted to fix that part of her too. So, He called her out, or rather asked who touched Him. He wanted her to step out openly, to not just have the faith for her healing, but to slap shame in the face by having the faith to be seen. He did not want her to continue to live the rest of her life unnoticed.

When she revealed herself, He confirmed what had happened and called her daughter. This was not just some random term of endearment. This is the only time Jesus called someone daughter in the New Testament. This tells us that this was a very intentional and specific word for her. We don't know her full story, but we can guess that before or throughout all the years of her affliction, she had been without affirmation, connection and cover. He called her daughter, and therefore reminded her of her place and her belonging. He made her whole.

How sweet is our Jesus? And He longs for the same for you. He doesn't want you to be satisfied with one aspect of healing when He paid for you to have everything. He doesn't want you to be ok with temporary relief when it's His desire to give you what is lasting and eternal. He wants you healed and whole.

How does this work? Think about the things in your life that you are petitioning Him for. What are you waiting for Him to accomplish? Healing is on the way to you and as soon as you cry out and let your heart and voice be heard He is coming your way. In this place we must also make sure that we continue to silence lies and break off the mindsets that keep us from entering into what He has made available to us. In the book of Numbers in the Bible we have a sobering example of what it looks like when we come into agreement with accusation and fear instead of faith and love. Twelve spies from the tribes of Israel were sent into the land that the Lord promised to give to His people. Victory was a done deal regardless of the giants and obstacles in the land. But because of their agreement with fear, ten of the spies led the people of Israel into unbelief and doubt. This exposed the old Egypt mentalities that were still within them. Instead of going immediately into the land, their disobedience and unbelief caused them to have to wander in the wilderness for 40 more years. What was supposed to be a temporary place of process turned into a generation of wandering. An entire nation was delayed from walking in the wholeness and abundance of the Lord because of the unbelief of a few.

My friend, let's not let the little distracting and tripping things in our lives keep us from the wholeness that God has promised for us. Hebrews 12:1 reminds us to throw off everything that hinders and the sin that so easily entangles. It's so easy to sit back and believe that our current state is all that there is and that there will never be an opening to what's been boxed around our lives. But it's not only in God's ability, it is in His heart to see you walk in complete freedom.

Prepare your heart to receive by faith what it is you're praying for. He is the God that can and will bless you abundantly but let me tell you, don't ignore the crumbs or the edges that you may find along the way. The crowd was so thick and intense that the woman with the issue decided that she would fight for His hem and believed that even a strand from His cloak could change her life.

I highlight this because you need to remind yourself of how powerful your God is. Just a strand of His garment, the edges of glory that He leaves in His wake, can bring healing. Or in the case of the Syro-Phoenician woman, a crumb off His table (Matthew 15:21-28 and Mark 7:24-29) did the same. If he did much with so little then all of Him is more than enough to bring your healing. But more importantly, to make you whole. The Lord delights in doing work in us from the inside out and letting the physical touches be icing on the cake. He can still heal even if someone doesn't want to be made whole like the case of the 10 lepers (Luke 17:11-19) but He wants to do an eternal work in all of us. That is what lasts and that is what positions us to then do work that lingers with the residue of His presence.

Linger in His presence. And as He comes, let Him call you out, let Him notice you and know you. He will reveal the hidden places in His way and in His timing that need to be brought to the surface. So that He can speak truth to you, replace the lies and empower you to walk in the whole truth of who you are meant to be. Those pieces that needed to be reclaimed may look different for different people. But the core is and will always be this. You are a Child of God.

Establish

1. What are the things in your life you know are in need of healing? Physically, mentally, emotionally?

2. As you consider those areas, ask the Holy Spirit if there is a deeper root that needs to be made whole. Is there a sin or struggle that has developed in your place of suffering that needs forgiveness and the finishing work of the cross?

Milk & Honey: Daughter

Daughter.

Beloved child of mine. Apple of my eye.

Focus of my eternal attention.

Destined for more than you can imagine.

If only you could see what I see.

I have made a place for you.

Not separate from me, not one of striving or stress.

But with me, within me, a place of finely tuned rest.

A place specifically designed for you.

My love is not general.

That is a term too loosely applied to my people.

You are my child, intricately made and intimately known.

I love all and love each individually.

You are seen by me although you think you go unnoticed.

You do not go unnoticed this day or any other.

Do not pass by without knowing this full well.

I am coming for you, dear child.

I am on my way to you.

Sent by a Father to His daughter.

In more ways than you can ever imagine.

I am walking a road to you crowded by distraction

but every seeming delay is only one step closer to my glory.

You shall be an instrument of it.

Playing the melody that I set forth before creation.

Turning the weapons that were turned against you
into tools of worship and wonder.
Bringing forth the new song that is being declared over the earth.
And I'm on my way to sing it with you.

Chapter Five: The Definition of Daughter

There are themes that circle around our lives over and over. As the years pass, we get another revelation, another layer stripped off of that thing that really is a core longing, a core place, a central mission and focus.

I wrote my first book Becoming His several years ago out of the overflow of that place. I realized that my life was spent seeking and searching for what it meant to belong. To have a safe place that I could run to and be fully me and fully free to be that quirky, crazy girl. Isn't belonging the longing of all of our hearts? Isn't it oftentimes what drives our behaviors and actions, sets our mindsets in motion to find that place where we can stand on steady feet?

Many times, we are grasping for outward affirmations, for the accolades and accomplishments that will determine who we are and where we are supposed to be. But at a certain point I got tired of assuming what I thought was a good fit. Let me tell you, as good as our roles and titles and positions can be, if they lead us away from our true source then they should be counted as counterfeit until alignment takes place. That was where I was. Out of alignment, getting placed off-kilter by circumstance and situations and the upbringing that was beautiful but was absent of a consistent father.

I needed to go back to the beginning. To the Father who started it all, to what His intentions were when He created us. This thought of "original divine intent" was something that stirred in me for many years and that was even vocalized more clearly when I helped write the vision for a women's conference started at my church. One ordinary day three of my co-workers and friends gathered at a coffee shop, brainstorming ways we could impact and encourage the young women that we led in weekly youth ministry. We came up with a concept and a name that summed up what we felt. After we presented this vision to our senior pastor it transformed into a conference for all women.

I was asked to write down a vision for this gathering and among many declarative words, I wrote that we needed to get back to the original divine intent of our heavenly Father. And to do so we needed a revolution, a She Revolution. To revolutionize our thoughts and get back to the heart of the Father. It's been amazing to see how the brainstorming and prayers and thoughts and words have expanded and spread under the leadership of our senior pastors. Joining with other voices into a consistent ministry and yearly conference that have affected the lives of thousands of women and their families.

The key to all of it is the core message and it is that we were meant to Seek the Embrace of our Father. This was made possible and paid for by the precious sacrifice of Jesus. In doing so He cleared the pathway and allowed us to become sons and daughters of the living God. To redeem what happened before and to give us a way to move forward in relationship.

This is what we all crave. In order to satisfy that longing we must come into agreement with what Jesus paid for and why He paid for it. He didn't give His life on the cross and resurrect by the power of the Holy Spirit for us to sidestep our new identity and position. 1 John 3:1 in the NIV says it out clearly for us: "See what great love the Father has lavished on us, that we should be called children of God."

Do you see the lavishing? Can you close your eyes and picture it? Do you see, taste and touch what He has poured over you? Sticky and sweet, lasting, lingering, His approval, His affirmation, His adoption of you as His daughter. Beloved, becoming more and more like Him. Belonging.

Our first and core identity is that we belong to Him.

I thought I would have it more figured out the older I became but I've realized that the older we get the more roles we take on. We become sisters, friends, we may become wives, we may become mothers, we may become grandmothers. We have roles that we fill in our homes, work, in the community. Sometimes along the way we forget that we had one title from the beginning and that was being HIS. And for us as women, that means His daughters. His baby girls.

Think about it. Every woman who has ever been born originates from the same place. We are all daughters; we are all someone's child. Even if we've been cared for and cherished, even if we've been neglected, even if we've been given up for adoption. We are all daughters no matter what other titles get added or taken away. When we lose focus on who we are and who we are meant to be, we begin to seek after and settle for counterfeits, for allusions of identity instead of the reality of who God made us to be.

So now assess where you stand. Look at your feet through the light of His word that is a lamp onto our feet (Psalm 119:105). Do you see His feet there as well? So close to you. His toes, His nail pierced feet touching your toes? Or are you far off, walking at a distance, off on a path that you wandered onto unintentionally or with much intention in mind. Where do you stand? Because the goal is to be close. Now that you know who He says you are, beloved, be where He is.

We must go back to the beginning if we want to release something around us that is lasting. If we want to cultivate in desolate and barren places fruit that is sustaining and sweet. You yourself may feel off, unhinged, off-kilter, caught off guard, left alone, not understood, misplaced, forgotten, unloved. You have now been reminded of His sweetness, you know that your healing is on the way, have loosed the lies and are working on becoming whole. We need to be reminded that as daughters we have a Father who specializes in forming and making us into exactly what we need to be. We now need to never forget what He thinks about us. And to believe wholeheartedly that He truly is a good Father. And He is really good at the embracing part, holding us, loving us and delighting over us like only our Creator- Father-God can.

Go Deeper into Identity

I realize that the things discussed in Part 1 barely scratch the surface for some of you. You are in need of even more insight and revelation to be positioned for complete wholeness within your identity in Christ. Jesus accomplished everything for us at the cross and now it is time for you to access it. As a co-heir, as a child of God there is nothing holding you back from doing so.

To find more resources that deal specifically with areas of Identity please visit www.milkandhoneywomen.com/identity

PART TWO

CULTIVATING INTIMACY

Part Two

"I have entered my garden, my treasure, my bride!
I gather myrrh with my spices and eat honeycomb with
my honey. I drink wine with my milk. Oh, lover and
beloved, eat and drink! Yes, drink deeply of your love!"
Song of Songs 5:1 NLT

"As the Father has loved me, so have I loved you. Now
remain in my love. If you keep my commands, you will
remain in my love, just as I have kept my Father's
commands and remain in His love. I have told you all this
so that my joy may be in you and
that your joy may be complete."
John 15:9-11 NIV

Filling the Vessel

There is a beautiful verse that details a wonderful promise that Jesus gave to a woman in the Bible. After she anointed His feet with oil and wiped them with her hair, He said about Mary of Bethany, that wherever the gospel is preached what she had done would be told in memory of her. Lasting legacy in the midst of lingering intimacy. Her life was more than an expensive perfume box. She positioned herself time and time again to receive into her vessel all the words and wisdom and presence and glory that Jesus had to pour out. She was a woman whose identity was established, so firm that she did not care how it looked when she sat at His feet. And in doing so, her vessel was filled and ready for when she needed to release a beautiful fragrance of worship. You see, before we can release the milk and honey of God's promise, we need to position ourselves to receive those promises. In this next part we will talk more about what it may look like to cultivate intimacy and take a peek into the lives of Mary and Martha of Bethany.

Her Moment of Intimacy

Mary, Martha and the death of Lazarus (Biblical Account found in John 11)

It was the look in her eyes. Martha knew instantly that something had shifted. Mary had sat with her head on her brother's shoulders for what seemed like days, refusing to leave his side, only moving when Martha took her place. She counted every breath, paid attention to every movement as they waited for word from the only One who could give them hope. And now, after waiting for a few days, there was no more time, hope was flying out of the window.

Martha saw the look she had been dreading since Lazarus' sickness took a turn for the worse. She had kept herself busy, greeting guests, talking to doctors, preparing meals. Doing anything to keep her mind distracted and her heart from the place she didn't want to go. She didn't think she could handle another loss, another disappointment. All they had was each other and now...she raised a shaking hand to her forehead. It was still covered in the grain she could not stop grinding even when others offered to help. She didn't think it would get this far, this bad. She was certain that her message would be received and the One they needed most would be here as soon as possible.

They had eaten together, laughed and teased and spent time in genuine friendship. He had even been corrective and honest with her, showing in His compassionate way how much He really did care. So where was He now? Why did He delay when their situation was so dire? He had healed others. Why wouldn't it be the same and even more so for their brother?

His dear friend Lazarus was sick and if He did not come soon, He would be...

"Dead! He's gone!" Martha felt the wail before the sound registered to her ears. She dropped her grain covered hand and crumpled to the floor next to her lifeless brother, her shock and disbelief zapping all the strength from her body. Mary inched closer, gripping her two siblings as best as she could and wept for the both of them.

* * *

The preparations were made and within a short matter of time Lazarus was laid in their family tomb. The sisters held each other tightly as the stone rolled into place. Its closure putting an end to the joy-filled and abundant life they once knew. They didn't have much but what they had always seemed multiplied by their brother's exuberant and generous nature. And now He was gone, and Martha didn't think she would ever smile again. In what way could she ever rejoice? As the crowd made its way back to the house Mary stayed hidden in the back rooms. The depth of her grief too heavy for words. Martha did her best as she always did, to speak and greet and eat the food others set before her. It was routine but as lifeless as her brother's body in that tomb. His place of rest for days now. And their dear friend still had not come.

On the 4th day, when someone tapped her on the shoulder, she almost didn't hear their words, she was so lost in her thoughts. "Say it again?" She turned toward a family friend, the one she had sent many days ago with a message to Jesus, asking Him to come, for the one He loved was sick. He looked at her, discomfort etched on His face. "He's here. Jesus is here." He said the last words a little louder this time, enough for those around to take notice. Martha heard the murmurs and waves of disapproval. Strength she didn't know she had moved her to her feet. She let her frustration propel her forward, past the wailers and neighbors and friends, out the front entry way and towards their gate where a small crowd gathered. There were so many words she wanted to say but she was deflated at just one look at His face. Instead the suffering of the last week overtook her and with pain choking her voice she said, "Lord if you had been here, my brother would not have died." She didn't understand what had kept Him but now she didn't even care. She wanted this fixed. She wanted things to go back as they were.

After speaking to her in only the way He could. Of resurrection and belief and hope she barely could conceive, He asked for her sister. Mary had hidden herself for days, her grief a shroud that covered her form, making her almost unrecognizable. She loved deeply and intimately, and the death of their beloved brother affected her greatly. And the absence of their friend broke her heart. But Martha knew that Jesus was the only one who could bring her out. One word from Him and her sister would be comforted. She thought of the time when she had tried to pit Jesus against her sister. In that moment she tried to pull Mary from her favorite place at the feet of Jesus. But now.

Martha didn't hesitate and hurried as fast as she could to tell her sister personally. Jesus was calling for her. She would bring her sister to Him this time and never pull her away from Him again. When Mary heard what she said, she stood up, trembling. Martha almost wept seeing the expression on her sister's face. So shadowed and gray, the light gone from her eyes. The spark that lit up a room diminished. Her own face must have looked similar because when Mary looked at her, her beautiful eyes welled with tears. "It's ok," Martha whispered, finding her voice amidst the emotion that threatened to break through. "He is here."

As soon as they made their way back to where Jesus stood, Mary crumbled. Some would have thought from weariness or fatigue. But Martha knew better. Her sister found her sweet spot, she found her favorite position again, at the feet of the one she loved. And in a broken tear filled voice she echoed the same words Martha shared. "Lord if you *had been here my brother would not have died."*

Jesus placed His hand on her head and looked around at all those mourning and grieving. His chest heaved with unspoken emotion and then He asked to see where Lazarus was laid. When they arrived at the tomb Martha watched their friend do something He had never done before in their presence. He wept. He knelt for a brief instant, His head in His hands, quietly grieving yet the emotion quaking through His body like thunder. After a few minutes He stood up and Martha saw an otherworldly intensity in His eyes as He set His gaze on Lazarus' tomb.

Milk & Honey: Crumbs

I need more of Him because the me without Him
is so incomplete,
just a shadow of His true intention for me.
Without Him there is no fullness of joy because there is no
fullness of me in Him.
Only pieces that I scatter, selling out my energy
to the highest bidder.
Leaving only the leftovers for Him…so I then become consumed,
in the day to day, meandering, surviving,
craving deeper connection
but settling for what's at the surface.
Yet in moments, those moments,
small insignificant seeds of attention,
when my intention supersedes my inventions…
I find crumbs.
Leading me, beckoning, giving tastes of what I am missing.
Crumbs that have fallen from His table,
that is overflowing for me.
Full of provision, of deep satisfaction, everything I need.
Crumbs.
They are not morsels meant to keep me
but to lead me to the source of me.
I need Him.

Chapter Six: A Well Worn Path

I have been fascinated by Mary and Martha for as long as I can remember as a believer. Growing up the Bible was never boring to me (ok except for Leviticus and anything that contained a lot of lists). I would read and begin to picture myself in those places, my imagination would flesh out the stories and bring texture to the black and white words I read. I became enthralled by the initial story of Mary and Martha because of the sweetness I saw displayed between Jesus and the sisters. These women, along with their brother Lazarus, were friends of Jesus and He visited them often. So often that a level of familiarity developed and soon Mary found herself more and more drawn to the words of Jesus, listening to what He said, sitting at His feet like the faithful student of a beloved rabbi.

Can you feel the warmth and closeness that this conveys? Can you see the joy of Jesus' smile and His tender gaze, looking around the room as He shared? Glancing every now and then at the devoted pupil at His feet. I don't believe every moment Jesus was at their house was a sermon or teaching. But for Mary, every word He said mattered. And I can see her storing those things up, treasuring them, as she did the oil in her alabaster jar.

It was this picture of closeness and intimacy with Jesus that drew me at an early age. I was captivated by a God who clothed himself in humanity and found pleasure in authentic and deep relationship with people— with women like you and me.

Stop and pause for a moment.

Consider what is being stirred in your heart right now. Maybe like me, you wish you could have a closer relationship with a parent. Or maybe you never even knew who yours was. Or perhaps you have been through numerous relationships or have been hurt by figures of authority. Maybe the pain of loss and disappointment has made you keep your distance from others. Whatever the case, we can all find ourselves in this story. Maybe not yet in the place of Mary. Some of us may be in the kitchen with Martha because we enjoy what we do, but don't yet know how to stop long enough to enjoy the Lord's presence. I think that many of us stand in the corner, too afraid to go over to where Jesus sits. Not wanting to be seen, not wanting to disrupt, not sure if we have permission. Wondering if this is the right season. Hiding behind our walls, safe within our control, not sure if we are fully wanted and able to be where He is.

But beloved do you see Him? He is looking your way. Smiling at you as if you are the only one in the room. Beckoning you to come closer. Patting the space next to His feet. Making room for you in a place where you previously may not have been allowed. A position from which He has the ability to lift you to your feet when it's time. Close enough to dry that tear from your eye and for you to rest in the nearness of His presence as you replace past lies for His truth. Do you see yourself there now? Good. Linger and let's continue.

Know this. There is always a time to be close, there is always the time for intimacy. It doesn't matter where you find yourself. You must be intentional to find Jesus in the midst and when you do, grab a hold of His feet. Position yourself so close. This is the model that Mary followed. She created a well-worn path up to the feet of Jesus. We don't know how many times she saw Him, but we do know what she did in the three instances we read about her in the Bible.

1. **Luke 10:38-42 – Sitting at the feet of Jesus during times of gathering and teaching.**
2. **John 11 – Falling to the feet of Jesus after the death of Lazarus.**
3. **John 12 – Kneeling at the feet of Jesus to anoint Him.**

Each time, Mary found herself at the feet of Jesus.

It was default for her—second nature that had become her true nature. She was constantly positioned to receive and to worship. Even when she didn't fully understand the circumstance, like we explored in the opening of this section. Mary's actions and posture moved me so much as a young woman because I thought, wow, she knew how to cultivate that sweet spot of friendship with Jesus. She knew where to go no matter the situation and even more significant was that she was welcomed there.

I'll be honest. There was a season after I married my husband that I didn't really know how to approach the Lord. My singleness had been such a catalyst into the arms of Jesus. That wilderness season for me was such a special time with the Lord and now that I was married it was like I didn't have the fuel to motivate me. I couldn't quite make out the path anymore. I had to reposition myself by placing Jesus as the central object of my affection again. It wasn't just about going through Him to get something that I wanted but agreeing fully that He was the One my heart was after. He was the promise and the present and the provision that I was seeking.

Think about the times you are at a gathering and you are in conversation with someone. But every so often their eyes dart around the room or they look over your shoulder for someone else. This lets you know pretty quickly that you are not necessarily the one they are looking for. Maybe you are an interesting filler or the step they need to take to get to who they are really waiting for. But whatever the reason, it's not fun to know that you are not the focus of their attention in the moment you are with them. And if we are being truthful with ourselves, we must ask, how many times have we done that to others? How many times have we done that to our Jesus? Used Him as a filler, as a steppingstone to get what are hearts are really after. Praying and wailing before Him to get whatever it is that we seek. Then when we receive that coveted thing, however good and godly it is, we don't even have the motivation to approach Him anymore. Because in all of our desire, the path we walked didn't lead to Him, rather He was the detour on our way to the destination we craved.

He is Lord of all, Savior of the world, King of the universe and this is how we often have treated Him. Oh, we were not the first and we will not be the last. But I'm so thankful that He takes in our human weakness, the frailty of our will and waits patiently for us to realize that He is the only one that matters. That no matter what we get or receive or how much we are blessed, the destination is Him. He is our true reward. This is what I missed even amidst all my years of growth and learning. My longings formed pathways that didn't lead me fully to Him after I received what I had desired. I had to repent of those ways, come into agreement with Romans 12 and transform my mind. My wonderful husband and new marriage were without doubt ordained by the Lord and gifts from Him. But I had to reposition my heart as I walked out what I prayed for and get my feet back on the path. A path that was a bit overgrown and untended in places. I had to get back on that trail that led me straight to Him.

This is what makes Mary such a hero to me. She didn't let anything deter her from finding herself next to Jesus according to what we see highlighted in scripture. Even when she had her doubts, or her hesitations in grief, once she got on that path she went straight to the place of intimacy. She went straight to the feet of Jesus.

This was more than coincidence. This was a specifically laid out pattern of a woman who was in love. A woman whose total dependence was on Jesus. She came near to Him in different seasons and situations. When we look at the story of her presented in the gospel, we see a moment of wonder, a moment of weeping and a moment of worship. These signified mountain highs and valley lows. But each time she found herself at the feet of Jesus. Her body coming into agreement with the position of her heart. And in those moments she learned a different aspect of Jesus' nature and character. Those revelations drew a response out of her that still teach us today. At His feet in wonder she discovered that time with Him was always the better choice.

At His feet in weeping she learned that Jesus truly cared for what she cared for and that He carried resurrection power. At His feet in worship, Mary understood that Jesus was more than a friend, He was their Lord, their King. He was the one worthy of the release of the fragrance of her worship. I wonder, dear sister, what the Lord has to teach you when you place yourself at his feet, no matter the situation. What is waiting to be poured into your heart during these sacred moments that you will in turn pour out over His feet in worship. There are treasures for you on the way to His feet.

This is the path we need to find ourselves on. Jesus is there, waiting and walking towards us. The question is whether we will find ourselves walking towards Him. Removing the obstacles on our path along the way—ignoring the distractions that try to remove us from the path to His presence. Mary's example should stir up great motivation in us. Because no matter what we face—no matter how dark the situation, how dry the season, how devastating the circumstance—there is a spot for us at the feet of Jesus. It is from this place that we receive all that we need, the place that turns the wonder and weeping and worship into fragrant offerings that minister to the heart of Jesus as He ministers to our own.

Cultivate

1. Take a moment today to sit before the Lord. With no agenda, no plan, just to listen. If needed put on a beloved worship song or play an audio passage from the Bible.

2. As you sit, my prayer is that you will find your way to a familiar path to His presence. And if there is not one, I pray that you would picture yourself at His feet and from there take in your surroundings. What do you see around you? An ocean, a beach, a mountain view, the tropics, a cozy chair, a garden?

Chapter Seven: Position over Performance

Platform. A word that has become synonymous with success and influence and the credibility to speak into a specific topic or area of interest. Platform can arise from various reasons. Maybe you are in a place in your career where what you do or what you have researched gives you the ability to speak into relevant areas. Maybe you have excelled in an area, your skills and talents giving you the ability to perform on the world's stage. And because of that you have a platform that allows you to make moves and shift momentum. Out of the overflow of this or out of the overflow of your family ties, friend connections, or entrepreneurial fame you have a platform. One that has steadily increased and expanded because of the amount of people who affirm your influence and follow what you do. This is platform.

According to the definition, it's a raised structure, a higher surface, a public statement[1] . We look at platforms large or small and at times allow that to determine what our position is or what we need to be positioning for. We want to increase our audience, expand our following, further our research, lift our intellect. We think that in order to make a move that has true momentum we need to have the platform that launches it. Or we mistakenly let a platform performance mentality determine what it is that we do or produce or release. I am here to tell you that there is much for you to do, much to release, much to produce and portray. But if it doesn't come out of a life in the right position before the Lord then what you do will only be temporary. It will not have lasting impact. I don't know about you, but I want what I do to leave a residue. Something not so easy to shake off or dismiss. Something not determined by time or trends but that is classic and lasting and eternal. This however does not originate from us. We may be a resource, but we are not the source. And aren't you glad?

But many times platforms are built, and performance is carried out that originate solely from us because we haven't take the time to position ourselves within our Source. We've forgotten that we are merely conduits and vessels, carrying the anointing from our place in the Lord out to those around us. You can run on battery power for only so long. At a certain point that temporary power will run out. But when you are plugged into the source, there is endless power available to you, running through you, bringing life to every place you touch.

Would you be willing to consider and ponder with me that your position trumps your performance and platform? That the power is in your position in Christ? That is the source for everything you need. It does not do away with those areas, but it gets them in the right place and alignment. Being in the right position, making the right choice to be where Jesus is makes everything else we do purposeful and effective and eternally impacting. It is a position of humility, submission, worship and full trust.

Trust. If you want to determine what position your heart is in, think about where your trust lies.

During our She Revolution women's conference many years ago we had a woman named Christa Smith speak to us during one of the evening sessions. She is the one who wrote the forward of this book. There are those moments whether in a corporate gathering, or smaller group study or in personal discussions with friends where words come out that mark you. They brand you with the fire of the Holy Spirit and you can't get away from the message—a sound, a phrase. The mark of burning coal that the Lord himself seems to be setting to your lips. This night was one of those nights for me.

Christa shared a powerful prophetic message about cycles and how there are things that we hold on to. Personality, habits, mindsets etc. that we are not willing to let go of. The Lord will always eventually bring us back to that thing, giving us opportunity to surrender it. It may be our attitude, our anger, our insecurity, our time management, whatever. She used the story of Moses in the Bible to illustrate how even in our success and ministry God wants to deal with these core aspects of our lives. Moses had issues with his speech and with walking in the confidence to speak out at the beginning of his call. At the end of his ministry, the Lord called him to speak to a rock, to bring forth water. Yet his insecurity came up again, triggered by the complaints of the people. So he struck the rock instead. Because of this, of not surrendering His fear and trusting the voice the Lord gave Him, He was not allowed to enter into the promised land.

I wept for most of the night. Even over dinner, as I sat with Christa and shared about what God was calling my family to, I couldn't keep the tears away. Because I knew the issue for me was trust. I didn't trust the Lord to cover me, to take care of me, to provide for me. I was afraid that we would make this move to Iceland and He would leave us hanging. It was then I realized that over and over, in so many situations in my life, the Lord was not just asking for my faith. Over the years this had become a given. I could put my faith in Him without too much of a fight. But He was asking for my trust. For me to view Him as the Father that He was. A Father that loved me so dearly and personally.

We get so caught up in what others are doing. We run around trying to please, trying to perform. The fear of man can be crippling. There were so many women especially in the Bible that had to fight through the words of others or the crowd to get to Jesus. When we are young, we have much faith in the presence of our parents. Of them always being there. But there may have been situations that occurred in your childhood that caused you to lose trust. And trust is a foundational need for all of us. According to Erik Erickson's stages of psychosocial development, trust vs. mistrust is the first foundational stage for human beings.[2] This stage is from birth to almost two years of age. A time when an infant should receive consistent, reliable and predictable care. Because babies cannot fend for themselves they are totally dependent on their caregiver. How they are taken care of during this stage determines whether they will build trust, confidence and hope or if they will deal with mistrust, anxiety and suspicion. This affects other relationships. For those of you who had situations that caused you to lose faith in those who were supposed to care for you, it can be hard to place your trust in others again and even in Jesus. The enemy does not want you to be confident in who you belong to because when you know who's got you and where to go then you really are unstoppable.

The call the Lord put on my family was definitely a big leap of faith with so many confessions and confirmations along the way. But in the midst—in the secret place— with everything else cleared away, it was just He and I standing feet to feet, toe to toe. In that place He asked me if I trusted Him. My response was what it was during times of surrender, submission, repentance and worship. I knelt at His feet. Not just placing the words of trust on my lips but positioning my entire spirit in His presence. Making the decision to relinquish my trust by putting it in the only One who could keep it safe.

> **"Those who live in the shelter of the Most High will find rest in the shadow of the Almighty. This I declare about the Lord: He alone is my refuge, my place of safety; He is my God, and I trust Him."**
> **Psalms 91:1-2 NLT**

The issue for you my sister, may not be trust. It may be a something else that you are holding so tightly to, afraid you will be disappointed again, afraid that you will fail. But remember, you are not the source. You are just a resource that must stay connected to the source. And it is in that secret place that the Lord wants you to kneel at His feet and surrender those things over.

In the previous chapter much was shared about Mary and how she always found herself at the feet of Jesus. No matter the season or circumstance she was there. We see the image of feet all over scripture. It is a significant position and posture that helps us to remain in Him like He desires us to. Being at the feet signifies humility and complete devotion, deference to the one whose feet you kneel by. It's also an act of servitude, of preferring the other to yourself. How interesting that in one of His last acts before He was crucified, Jesus knelt down to wash the feet of His disciples. Showing them in that act His care and love and devotion for His people and His desire for them to be clean and free. This position became a platform that spoke loudly of God's heart towards mankind and what Jesus came to do.

When you are in the right position with Him, whatever you do becomes a platform that showcases the glory of God. Here are some things to consider and questions to ask yourself when thinking about your posture.

The position of your heart (What is your motive?)
- o   **What are you wanting the outcome to be?**
- o   **What are you trying to produce?**
- o   **What do you want to happen?**

The positioning of your beliefs (What do you believe to be true? Really True.)
- o   **David believed He could take down Goliath.**
- o   **Joshua and Caleb believed that they could enter the land and defeat the enemy.**
- o   **Mary believed that Jesus's words and His presence were worth her attention and devotion.**

The positioning of your actions (What are you doing about what you believe?)
- o   **David refused to wear armor that didn't fit, took out His**

slingshot and rushed to kill the enemy.

o   **Joshua & Caleb obeyed and spoke boldly even when it didn't make sense to others.**

o   **Mary placed herself at the feet of Jesus in every single situation, recognizing that He was the source of all she needed.**

When we know Jesus, we are positioned in Him as children of God like we discussed in the first part of this book. But now, the positioning is really about remaining. Allowing ourselves to remain in Him and therefore remain in intimacy with Him. Cultivating a deep and close friendship with the Lover of our souls. You don't have to be afraid in this place. We don't have to be ashamed or shy or nervous to enter. In every day life there are times a bit of shyness comes on me and even when others invite me into their spaces it takes me a while to overcome my hindrances. In my mind, I don't want to inconvenience or to come at the wrong time. Or what will I say? What will I talk about? Any other ambiverts operate in a similar way? You love being with people but don't mind your times of solitude either? This comes into play so many times here in Iceland. My hesitations become magnified because I don't speak the language well so it's not just about what I will say but how will I say it? Yet, the position I take in Christ, of choosing to remain in Him, being confident of His love, keeping my spirit in that position of humility and surrender actually then catapults me to step out when it's time to be bold as I speak. Or at least try to.

Remaining in Jesus—sitting at His feet—is not a step back but it actually comes into agreement with the definition of platform. Because when we position ourselves in Him we agree in the Spirit that yes, we are actually seated with Christ, in heavenly places. What we go after in the flesh can actually be accomplished more effectively when we go after it in the Spirit too. This is the place of deep relationship, where we receive insight and strategy, beautiful thoughts and creative ideas. This is how we can cultivate the sweet spots no matter where we are. We stay connected to the source and because we are drenched in His love, His oil, His milk, His wine, His honey—we become vessels that release that prophetic provision wherever we walk. Whoever we talk to. We release the fragrances that shift the atmosphere around us. Walking out Holy Spirit anointed strategies that dismantle strongholds. When you operate from this place you understand that your position in Him is way more powerful than the performance you do without Him. It is the being still in Him that Psalm 46:10 speaks of, being still and letting Him do what He does best. Exalt Himself among all the nations. Exalt Himself among all the people of earth.

We can position ourselves with Him in our wonder and in our times of weeping however that looks like. But the quickest way is through our worship. If you were able to peek into my apartment on an average morning you would see me busily bustling about after getting my kids to school and my husband off to his assignments for the day. If I didn't have a meeting or radio show to prepare for I would be cleaning, doing laundry, putting away toys and the remnants from the morning rush. I would have music or a teaching on blast, remembering that this routine is not just a bother or a burden, it is my worship. A stewarding of what I've been given and knowing that my care for my family is a sweet fragrance to my King. Then you may see me find a good song. Turn it up loudly and then ask the Lord if He would like to dance. I would move my feet on the living room rug that is *supposed* to be cream, but hashtag kids, spinning and grooving and incorporating various moves from the 90s as I laugh and dance and worship my Jesus. I find that those moments help me move into my positioning with joy, setting a foundation for my day and launches me out freely from the mercy that approached me with the dawn.

There is no better platform then that. The one that is created between you and your Creator. He takes all of those things that we do in response to Him, lets it seed the sky and then pours out blessing and favor and insight and revelation into our imperfect but treasured vessels. And most of all, He pours himself into us from that place of abiding. Pushing out what doesn't look like Him. Filling us with what we need for wherever He needs us to be. Public or Private. Large or small. Followed or not. Find your position sister, tuck yourself into His side, nestle down at His feet and then watch as He sets you up, spins you around, setting in motion something beautiful from you.

Cultivate

1. Remember our talk of Identity in the previous section? Who are you? One of the best ways to ground yourself in your position is to remember who you are over what you do. The doing is important but who you are is what creates the root systems that dig deep into Jesus.

2. Find a piece of paper, journal, or a page of this book and draw a tree with long and wide roots. Don't worry, no one will judge how you draw. Thinking about who you are and then what you do, what labels need to go on those roots? What does it look like for you to abide in Christ? What in your life keeps you anchored to the Rock of Christ?

Milk & Honey: Personal

Let's take it personal,
move from the crowd to the kitchen table.
Move from waiting for a movement to engaging in the moments
that move us.
Moving us from inaction and viewing things from the sidelines
to playing the role we were created to.
In spotlights and in solitude. In boardrooms and in ballrooms.
In the waiting and in the birthing.
Let's take it personal.
Let's not wait for the crowd to follow, but let's choose to go
because He said so. Let the whisper of the Father in our ear be
enough to get us going, leading to momentum in our seeking for
the more that awaits. The depth that is ours for the taking.
Let's make it personal,
no longer shifting the blame or the fame to someone else.
Content to sit in our indifference and insecurity.
Afraid to move lest we be seen,
restless in our staying because we are not abiding.
There is power in my agreement with Heaven.
I don't need a platform to be positioned at the feet of Christ.
He paid the price to seat me in heavenly places,
to move mountains in a minute that might have taken a
millennium to shift.Let's shift our focus, let's be led by the Spirit.
Let us step out when He says so, let us be grounded in humility

when He says go, understanding that the further we see
the deeper in Him we must be.

Chapter Eight: Calling out the Call

"Oooo, she called you out!"

I don't know if you have ever used that term or had someone use it in relation to you. But I think we are all pretty confident that when that expression is thrown out there it means that someone has been put in their place. Hidden information has been shared or someone is potentially laughing at your expense. Sometimes it can be a funny expression shared between genuine friends but there are times it is used in a not so positive way. The nature of the message is determined by the heart and intention of the messenger.

I shared in the first part about the friend of mine who shared some pretty weighty messages with me. Things that she had received from the Lord and passed along to my heart. One of them took place right after the Lord roared away the lies that I had come into agreement with. His encounter with me later prepared me to receive what may have been otherwise hard to hear. I wasn't being called out by my friend from a heart of jealousy or insecurity. She didn't do so pridefully or even with pressure, she was simply being obedient to the Lord and stepped out boldly and humbly with her words. I couldn't hide among my baggage or go away unnoticed. I was being called out from among my fear and the lies that I believed. I was being called out to Jesus. To trust Him with my family and in turn trust the mantle and anointing He had placed on my husband.

My sweet sister in Christ had to make a decision when she felt the impression from the Lord. Either she could sit on those words longer than she was supposed to or she could step out in courage and call me to more. I'm so glad she did the latter. I'm so thankful I was able to see myself through the eyes of my Father. To know how much He loved me and that this was a divine intervention for me. I believe He was so done watching fear ravage my life and halt forward movement. He came to me as a lion to redeem the past, roar away the lies and then sent a faithful discerning sister to speak truth in love to me. Milk and honey truly flowed from her tongue that night as tears flowed from my eyes. I wept and repented and had the tools I desperately needed to be wide open honest with my husband. This shifted the course of my family, all because I was called out. I am forever grateful.

As we discussed in the last chapter you don't need a platform to be positioned in a place to speak. Rather it is your positioning in Christ that gives you the authority and anointing to speak out. Your voice and words may not look or sound like anyone else's. But I promise you that the Lord has given you an area that He wants you to speak into, people around you to encourage. They may be as close as your family or children, your siblings and parents, your friends and community. Or sometimes, in a season of transition or in times when you may be more isolated than you wish to be, you need to stand in the mirror and declare the words of the Lord over yourself. Call yourself to level up to what the Lord thinks of you and get lower, get your roots deep in Him.

We see all throughout the Psalms that David was no stranger to calling himself out and encouraging himself. He did this especially in his deepest and darkest moments when it seemed like there was no one else for him to turn to. Our words are not only impactful if they land on someone else. The Lord may be asking you to believe enough to speak words of life and empowerment over your own self. If we are called to love our neighbors as ourselves then it seems beneficial to love ourselves first by being positioned in the unshakeable love of the Father.

This confidence that we get from Him then gives us a firm foundation to launch our words from.

I find it interesting that when Jesus finally arrived at Bethany and the house of His friends, it was Martha that approached Him first. The tables were turned. She was the one who got close first and Mary is the one who stayed away initially. We don't know exactly why but things had shifted. This should show us that someone's strength in one season may not be the same in the other. I love this example because it helps me remember that Mary was not perfect. She had a consistent pattern and posture, but she also dealt with her own doubts and disappointments.

So, as Jesus approached it was Martha who took the first step towards Him. It may be that she decided she didn't want to miss her opportunity to be close to Jesus. The first time we meet Martha she is calling her sister out publicly because she is upset that her sister is not helping her in the kitchen (Luke 10:38-42). I want to camp out here for a bit. And I want to tread carefully and in humility. As a church and as women we need to watch our own words and motives. Remember the whole positioning thing? Martha was doing a good work. She was preparing food for the disciples and Jesus. But because her heart was most likely out of alignment and positioned in what I would call insecurity, she no longer had contentment in what she was doing. She used that moment to agree with rejection and assumed that somehow Jesus didn't care. She wanted Him to tell Mary to get up from His feet to help her in the kitchen. She was attempting to call her sister out and in doing so, call her sister away from the presence of Jesus.

Man. When you place it in the context of our lives and even the modern church you might just begin to hear the echoes of her words in the hallways, in the backrooms, in the sanctuary, at the altar. What have we allowed to get in the way of true freedom? And if you listen close enough, maybe you can hear Jesus call your name, loving correction on His tongue. Asking you why you are worried about so many things, things that don't really matter when the only person that matters is in the room. Or maybe it's this. We have gotten so caught up in our traditions and culture and activity that we haven't even realized that Jesus is not in the room. I spoke of this a bit in my first book Becoming His[1] in the chapter about Martha:

> *Martha made a decision in the midst of her distraction. A similar decision to ones we make in our homes, in our schools, in our jobs, in our ministry, in whatever leadership role the Lord has given us stewardship over. We get so caught up in our roles that are expectations shift from why we are doing what we do to what others should be doing in response to what we do. Often we get so distracted with the "doing" that we forget the "being". We miss our moments to just be with Jesus. We forget that nothing else matters when Jesus is in the room. When our focus is off of Him, we lose perspective on what really matters in our daily interactions and don't use our gifts and talents the way the Holy Spirit intended.*
> (Becoming His, pg. 178)

This story hits home for me because the Lord used it to open my eyes to my own prideful ways. Years ago, I was on the leadership team of our church's college ministry. It was a great season where we had lots of people in college and the early stages of their careers and families join us. Many who came were new believers or ones that were still searching. There was one gathering where I was sitting towards the back, two rows behind a young woman that had been coming for a few weeks. She was one of those new believers. As we sat listening to the message, I noticed that she was braiding the hair of the girl in front of her. I was annoyed that she would be doing anything else but listening to the message. I tapped the shoulder of a young women right in front of me and asked her to get the attention of the hair braider. When she looked at me, I put on my sternest "leader" face and shook my head, telling her to stop. I felt completely justified in my correction and how I called her out.

It wasn't until a few weeks later that I noticed I wasn't seeing her show up anymore. I didn't have her phone number and to be honest had forgotten her name. Years later as I began to dig deeper into the story of Mary and Martha, I realized with horror that all this time I thought I was living my life as a Mary, positioning myself at the feet of Jesus. And I think in some instances and seasons I was. But in this situation and probably others I was a misguided Martha. Calling my sister out. And in doing so I called her away from the community she was forming relationship with. I called her away from the presence of God she was encountering in our services. When I think of her it still brings a tear to my eye. I repented to the Lord for my actions and I still pray consistently that me calling her out that day didn't turn her away from the Lord completely.

That was an eye opening moment for me. One that I will never forget. It gave me a new perspective of sisterhood and what it really means to call someone out. We like to use that phrase, especially when we are about to go off on someone or want to go off. We will call that person out and set them straight. But my sisters, we must make sure that we do so out of the overflow of abiding in Christ. Out of the right position. Because of my pride I called a sister out in the wrong way. Because of Martha's own issues she called her sister out. But I love how Jesus took care of it and defended Mary without bringing shame on Martha. He spoke the truth in love to her. Acknowledging her worries, letting her know that He cared but making sure she knew that Mary had made a choice that was more important and lasting.

So fast forward to the tomb and Martha rushing out to meet Jesus. She wasn't going to miss her moment this time, no matter the circumstance. And in this instance a beautiful thing happened. After Martha talked with Jesus, Jesus asked about her sister. And in a wonderful moment of redemption Martha went to Mary and called her out. But this time she called her away from her isolation and loneliness, she called her away from her doubts and disappointment. She called her out and called her to Jesus. This story should shift all of our perspective and give us hope. We have been given a mandate to call out our sisters and brothers and friends and children and community and even ourselves. But the mission is to call out the call in others. We need to make people aware that they are being called out because Jesus himself calls for them. We are these sticky messengers, these vessels of His love and grace and mercy. We are meant to position ourselves in Christ, to make Him our one thing, our good choice that will not be taken away. And in doing so we will see what the Father is doing, we will hear how He is calling His children home and we will release our voices and the sounds of our lives to call our siblings back to Jesus.

We don't call out to make ourselves feel better because of what someone else is doing or because we are afraid and intimidated. We call out people, men and women into who they are meant to be. That is who we are as women. We are birthers, we are doulas, we are midwives, calling out, pushing forward! And not calling them to ourselves but to Him.

It is to call them out into who God created them to be. It's to say come here, get a better perspective, come get closer to what's available to you. It's about being His, belonging to Him and taking others there.

God is wanting us to turn the moments that we are His into momentum that changes our core and lifestyles, allowing us to constantly stay His, remaining in Him. In all that we do for Jesus we can't forget to be *with* Jesus. We don't know what season people are in, how they are trying to position themselves to be His. In one moment, Mary was there, she was at His feet but in another moment, she needed to be reminded.

Did that moment at Jesus feet when she was called out to help, hinder her response when her brother died? Was it an open door the enemy used to bring shame and isolation? It was still her own response, her own responsibility, but we need to ask ourselves, what kind of atmosphere are we cultivating in our sphere of influence? In the place the Lord has us planted in? Jesus defended Mary but we don't need to help the enemy in bringing accusations against others.

This time at her brother's death, even though the important miracle was the resurrection of Lazarus, I believe Jesus had something additional in mind. An opportunity for Martha to level up and walk in redemption. Martha draws Mary back out to Jesus and leverages her important role with her sister to call her to Jesus. She ensures that their home remains a safe place of sisterhood, freedom and worship. They were meant to do life together, strengths and weaknesses, passion and position working in unity to create an atmosphere that Jesus was welcome in and from where Jesus could influence those that came through their village.

Could it be that when Martha called her sister Mary out *to* Jesus that it empowered her later to pour the perfume on Jesus' feet? Could it be that Mary was confident to perform one of the most powerful acts of worship done by a human being because of the encouragement of her sister? This was part of Mary's call. And that calling needed to be called out.

The calling needs to be called out in people all around us. We were all called to be with Jesus. We don't need to underestimate the power of our encouragement, especially among our sisters. We need to reach out and say Jesus is calling for you! In the midst of darkness and grief and pain, we are called to be those spiritual doulas coming alongside, bringing support, reminding women that in the highs and lows we belong to Him.

There may be a season that you have to lay yourself down at the feet of Jesus and you will need women around you to speak life over you, to cover you and not halt the process that Jesus is taking you through. And then there will be another season that you will be serving and giving. But in that season, you can serve and give with anointing because you have been at the feet of the anointer, Jesus the Anointed One.

We are blessed to have women in our lives who sit at the feet of Jesus, prioritize His presence and are saturated with the provision that flows from Him. This is the type of sister who called me out. I was so thankful that the Lord encountered me in that way that night. He used a sister in Christ to lovingly speak hard truth to me. She called me out in the Holy Spirit, and it was not to put shame or condemnation on me. She revealed the darkness in me that I couldn't name and stirred conviction and repentance in me. She called me out to Jesus. This was a defining moment. This was the ripping off of the old wineskin to make way for the new. God was preparing to pour something into my life, and I needed my hands open to receive it, no longer clenched in fear. I was called out because God was calling us to Iceland.

Cultivate

1. Has there been a time when you called someone out in the wrong way? How did you feel? Were you able to make it right?

2. Has there ever been a time when you called someone out in the right way? How did you feel? Have you seen the fruit from it?

3. Is there an area in your life that someone has called you out on? Do you feel like it led you closer to Jesus?

4. Is there something that you know the Lord is calling you to that you are afraid to say yes to?

Chapter Nine: Moving with what Moves Him

Wasn't it Moses who said, if your presence doesn't go with us, we do not want to go? This type of relationship doesn't settle for counterfeits. When you've tasted the reality of His presence anything less is sour and unsatisfying. It's the cup that we drink from that doesn't quench our thirst. It is the five husbands of the Samaritan woman versus Jesus who had lasting living water that He wanted to give her. That He makes available for us all.

There are so many causes and opportunities that we can get involved in. Because of the technology of our day, a project geared toward your passion can be no more than a fingertip away. You can be a generous person, a social activist and an advocate for justice right from the comfort of your living room. It is easy to be moved by what moves us and stirs our emotions. But are we willing to be moved by what moves Him?

When I know who I am in Christ and operate out of my identity and out of the overflow of intimacy with Him, the things I then do are not just born out of my abilities. They are anointed supernaturally to shift things in the physical but also penetrate the spiritual realm. I believe it's the Lord's desire and it should be ours too, to not just bring physical change but for there to be eternal impact. Am I carrying an anointing that will affect many generations to come and the generations within my spheres of influence? Have I been around the anointed one so much that what is on Him rubs off on me?

When Mary poured the oil on Jesus, she was so close that the oil naturally remained on her. The fragrance also spread to those in the room, her sphere of influence. They then had to come to grasp with their own surrender, their own extravagant worship or lack thereof. Her worship released something to Jesus that automatically released back on her. It is the beauty of the abiding, the remaining, the position of being settled in Him.

It's not about striving to make something happen, but embracing the sacred. Being faithful in the secret, pursuing His pleasure and waiting for the timing of the Lord. For when He calls you out and pours His oil of anointing. The oil that the prophet Samuel poured on David in the Old Testament did not just anoint him for kingship but was the stronghold breaker, the ability for his songs to help bring deliverance, the catalyst for him to slay a giant. I also can't fail to mention that David was anointed because of how he positioned himself in hidden places.

David was not just anointed for a platform ministry even though that would come in its proper timing. In the future he would get to be in a place of major influence or as I will share about in the next part of the book, macro influence. David remained faithful in his daily tasks, shepherding His flock, finetuning his skills, cultivating worship and staying in relationship with the Lord. He had a sweet spot of anointing that overflowed into everything that he put his hands to. It is this positioning that allowed him to step boldly to the giant Goliath, declare the victory of the Lord with his words and then carry it out with his actions.

I believe that David is one of the greatest examples of being moved by what the Lord was moved by. He had a deep sense of justice and wanted to honor God's heart. This even came into play when he made huge mistakes concerning Bathsheba and her husband Uriah. He came into agreement with God's heart and God's justice when he was called out by the prophet Nathan. He longed for a clean and pure heart so that

He would not be hindered in following after the Lord. It is this David that the Lord said had a heart like His.

This is what we must be after. The heart of God. Not being moved by our own inclinations or opinions or timetable or circumstances. No. We must come into agreement with who He is, what He says and what He longs to do. This is the type of relationship that brings lasting change. A kingdom was established on this type of intimacy as in the example of David. With Mary of Bethany, out of her intimacy Jesus said that wherever the gospel was preached, what she had done would be told.

Mary's actions had eternal and lasting significance. She poured out the oil of her worship being moved by what was moving her savior. It is interesting that Jesus himself said that what she did was preparing Him for His burial. We don't know how much she knew about the significance of her act, but we do know that it was a prophetic one and that she positioned herself in response to the purpose of Jesus on the earth. Jesus came to give himself for us and in doing so paid the bride price for us all. His bride the church. Consider the following scriptures and how they beautifully relate to what Jesus came to do for us and what Mary did.

"I will betroth you to me forever; I will betroth you in righteousness and justice, in love and compassion." Hosea 2:19 NIV

And then Song of Songs 1:12 says this beautiful prophetic phrase:

"While the king was at His table, my perfume spread its fragrance."

You see, your actions, your movements, your worship—is all in response to what has already been done for us. It is a natural outpouring and overflow of movement based on what our Lord is moved by. It is stepping into the same rhythm that was modeled to us by Jesus when He said:

> **"Very truly I tell you, the Son can do nothing by himself, He can do only what He sees His Father doing, because whatever the Father does the Son also does." John 5:19 NIV**

Jesus modeled this for us, setting into motion this beautiful flow and harmonic relationship. The Father moved in response to His love for us sent His Son. The Son moving in response to the Father brought healing and deliverance and salvation to us. The Holy Spirit in response to the Son baptized us in fire, bringing boldness and comfort and teaching us the ways of Jesus. We then respond to the Spirit that is moving and leading within us and operate in the ways of our Father, coming into agreement with Holy Spirit to bring Jesus into every situation.

We need to practice our agreement with the Holy Spirit in all areas so that when we end up in desert places or on public stages we know how to respond. We are meant to lean on the leading and guidance and friendship of Holy Spirit.

> **"The Spirit and the Bride say, "Come!"**
> **Revelation 22:17a**

This is what happens out of the overflow of our agreement, which can only be birthed out of intimacy. When we operate this way, we are positioned to release influence that releases the power and authority of Jesus into our lives and the lives of those that we come in contact with.

He wants us. Heart mind and soul positioned in His presence, positioned in the flow of His heart toward us. The us that He fully knows and fully loves. We must fight the things that fight our intimacy. We must not be moved by the opinions of people but by the thoughts God thinks of us. I heard a minister named Dano McCollum share something powerful during a teaching time for current and future missionaries. He reminded us that the Bible says that God's thoughts over us are as numerous as the sand on the seashore. Of course, we know that sand itself is almost immeasurable. How can we even count a handful of sand? The world is estimated to have over 7 quintillion (7.5 x 10^18) grains of sand.[1] We can't even conceive of that in our natural minds. If those are the thoughts He has over me then that means there are so many scenarios and plans and purposes and affirmations waiting for us to pull down. Waiting for us to obtain in the secret place with Him. That's what the price was paid for. This wonderfully sweet and powerful friendship with God. Jesus brings us into full relationship with Him so that out of the overflow we see things shift. Out of the overflow we see atmospheres change and our works then become anointed agents of change. Lights in darkness come from the ones close to the flame.

It is my hope that as believers we don't just want to take up causes because they look good or make sense or because we feel pressured to. Even in the anointing that took place from Mary, Judas complained that the perfume could have been sold and money given to the poor. But interestingly Jesus wasn't moved by that, at least not in that moment. He even said, "The poor you always have with you, but you don't always have me." In that moment, like the other times Mary found herself at Jesus' feet, the important and better choice was choosing Jesus. It's not that Jesus did not care for the poor or their issues, it's just that in what Mary did something was being released that would anoint and prepare Jesus, who would in turn anoint and prepare us to do His works. He was positioning His people to operate in truth, authority, anointing, and power. Then the poor could be cared for and ministered to according to the heart of God.

Choosing Jesus as our first ministry and allowing ourselves to be moved by Him and moved by what moves Him allows us to be activists that are anointed and timely. Not only making moves in the physical but breaking chains in the spiritual. When we anoint Jesus with our worship and extravagance, we release a fragrance that shifts things around us, setting things in place, challenging and changing hearts, putting our Jesus on display. Let us be positioned close to what He cares about. Let us be moved by what moves Him. To cultivate relationships of intimacy and friendship that allow Him to cry out for what we cry out for, and for us to grieve over what grieves His heart.

Cultivate

"You have captured my heart, my treasure, my bride. You hold it hostage with one glance of your eyes, with a single jewel of your necklace. Your love delights me, my treasure, my bride. Your love is better than wine, your perfume more fragrant than spices."
Song of Songs 4:9-10 NLT

1. Do you feel delighted in? Take some time to ask the Lord what delights Him about you. This may seem like a strange exercise but pull out a journal, a blank piece of paper, the notes app on your phone. Write down the words that come to your mind as you set your thoughts on Him and ask Him this question. What He says may surprise you, it may even delight you.

2. Do you know what moves the Lord? Going through the same process, ask the Lord what moves His heart and how you can be positioned to move with Him. Write it down.

Milk & Honey: I write

I write because at a certain point I tire of just telling
how to do something.
Letting my words be constrained and contained
within a box of just information,
to sit on a shelf unattended and forgotten.
Never released into the atmosphere of your life and into the sky
where kingdom can rain down.
I tire of telling something that I am not willing to finish,
not willing to plant and then dig up,
letting the roots down deep,
letting the fruit soar out and high.
Letting you and I taste and see that the Lord is so good
and so sweet and so needed.
I write so that I can show, not just tell.
Write stories that capture you and pull you in to testimony.
Let you breathe it in, taste of it,
be saturated in the experience of what God is doing and can do.
Calling things that are not as though they are,
writing the stories that I want to see.
Painting a masterpiece that invites you into the story
that is meant for you to color
with the image of beauty He has placed on you.
I want to write prophetically,
prose that proposes and ponders on mysteries

only available to those who will choose to access
the riches of eternity.
That declares what is not into what can be,
speaking forth with a breath of creative power
what in fact should be, on earth, as in heaven.
In this dirt bring in heaven.
So. I write. So that it shall be.

Chapter Ten: Unboxing Beauty

Let's review a bit. Influence starts with worship. Worship takes place within intimacy and intimacy is cultivated when your identity is established, when you know who you belong to. What kind of influence you release is determined by what you are inspired and influenced by. You become what you behold, you release what you receive.

Mary received something from Jesus that she was willing to give everything for. She had a beautiful gift in the form of her box that could be used as the start of a beautiful marriage in the future. But instead of giving it to another man she gave it to the one that mattered above all else.

> "Here a dinner was given in Jesus' honor. Martha served, while Lazarus was among those reclining at the table with Him. Then Mary took about a pint of pure nard, an expensive perfume; she poured it on Jesus' feet and wiped His feet with her hair. And the house was filled with the fragrance of the perfume. But one of His disciples, Judas Iscariot, who was later to betray Him, objected, "Why wasn't this perfume sold and the money given to the poor? It was worth a year's wages." He did not say this because He cared about the poor but because He

was a thief; as keeper of the money bag, He used to help himself to what was put into it. "Leave her alone," Jesus replied. "It was intended that she should save this perfume for the day of my burial. You will always have the poor among you, but you will not always have me." John 12:1-8 NIV

Of course, the enemy was there stirring up trouble as usual. Bringing accusation that was unfounded but seemed sensible. The choice between giving to the temporal need and anointing the eternal was presented but Jesus made an interesting statement. He made it clear that the poor were always going to be a part of community and therefore should always be taken care of. Jesus wasn't saying to never give to the poor, but He was saying that Mary recognized the power in a moment and took advantage of it. Tomorrow they could give to the poor, and maybe yesterday they should have but today, today, Jesus was in the room. And it was Mary's act that Jesus said would be told about her wherever the gospel was preached. That is eternal.

Because it matters. The choices you make, the beauty you release matters. Not just in the way of what others think or feel or how they respond. But because when you *do* in the overflow of He in you, you reflect a part of His nature that was needed on the earth. You cause Him to smile in a way that we may not have experienced. What favor has He poured on you that we need splashes of? What love has He lavished on you that needs to trickle into your streets and neighborhood? Your fingerprint of worship releases a fragrance that fills the rooms you find yourself in.

Let's not put limits on what the Lord can use to bring Him glory and honor. He can use whatever vessel He chooses. Your fingerprint of worship does not depend on the validation of others. The extravagance of what you release is for His glory. When we take the boxes off of our unique beauty and anointing, a fragrance is released that will fill every room you walk through. What happens with it is not your responsibility, the pouring it out on Jesus is. That's the place your worship belongs. If it gets poured out for the admiration of people, then you have missed the whole point of why you were created.

What we do for the approval of people will only get us so far. What we do to please the Lord and capture His attention are what position us to make lasting eternal impact. This is the beauty that matters and that cannot be contained by circumstances. Sometimes the hard circumstances themselves, the season of suffering that we didn't ask for, are what the Father turns for His glory. The pressure and the crushing release a fragrance that illuminates His story being written in you. It's a scent that lingers, a beauty that causes the Lord to draw close and lean in.

We can see this illustrated in the story of Naomi and Ruth. You can read more in the book of Ruth but in it you see two women, joined first by a wonderful life event, the marriage of Ruth to Naomi's son. But then almost torn apart by another shared tragedy. The death of Ruth's husband and Naomi's son. But what bonded them together was the decision Ruth made out of the overflow of this terrible circumstance. And I believe that decision was influenced by the beautiful fragrance that lingered in Naomi's life. Even when she saw her story as bitter and tragic, marred with death and loss, there was a sweet serenade that remained. One that drew Ruth closer. Closer to God and eventually closer to the man that would be their redeemer.

Sometimes beauty is the most evident in times of great darkness and turmoil. It's the rose growing through concrete, determined to not be hindered. Tender and delicate but unable to be shackled by any prison. Because let me tell you, no one can stay in their prison when the King comes near unless they choose to. And when the King is drawn in by the beauty of your worship, He has this wonderful way of breaking off what tried to break you down.

"Let the king be enthralled by your beauty; honor Him, for He is your Lord." Psalm 45:11 NIV

Your beauty and the beauty that you release is not defined by others.

Jesus is the one who calls it beautiful; you do a beautiful thing because you do it to Him and for Him. Pouring back out what He poured into you at creation. Jesus said that wherever the gospel was preached what Mary had done would be told because it was what Jesus was coming for. To bring reconciliation back to the Father, to show us how close and intimate He wants to be with us. Mary was walking in her true calling, one who ministered to the heart of Jesus. She literally broke the box of what her life was supposed to be defined by and decided that Jesus was worth receiving all she had. When we point our worship toward Jesus and allow Him to be in the center of all we do, our works become more. They become worship and it is beautiful to behold.

What places our worship in boxes in the first place? I think a lot of times we are so wrapped up in the fear of man that we are looking for permission. I struggled so much with this when we began our second year in Iceland. I cried out to God to define my role for me in this new season but the thing was, he had already done that. It was found in my worship. And my core fingerprint of worship has always been the words I write down. One particular week I was really putting this before the Lord because I didn't know if I had permission to write like my heart was leading me to. I didn't want it to take away from our mission or to be viewed negatively by others. That following weekend we attended a gathering with several pastors and leaders from across Iceland. The couple sitting next to us were missionaries from England who have been in Iceland for many years. During a break, the wife began to ask me questions about my time here, my family, how I was doing. Suffice it to say I was in tears. She had been in a similar position and knew where I was at. And then she said these words that poured refreshing onto my weary heart, "You need to keep writing." I looked at her in awe because this was what I had been specifically praying for a few days before. "You need to write and you don't need permission." Those words were a balm to me and by the time we left the gathering the next day, I was so thankful that the Lord used her to encourage me. But that wasn't the end.

During this same weekend, my home church in Huntsville, The Rock Family Worship Center, was having their yearly women's conference. This same conference I mentioned earlier in the book. So I had been a little more emotional that weekend anyway thinking of all my friends gathered there. I missed home in the states but the encouragement I received from this sweet missionary had buoyed my heart. When we were almost to our apartment, I began receiving messages from friends at home. On text, facebook messenger, through Instagram. Apparently, one of the speakers at the conference, Jennifer Toledo, had a word for me during her message. For me, thousands of miles away. From the stage she said that she felt the Lord has sent me to Iceland to write. That whatever was over here was what I needed to begin to release more books. I was once again in awed shock and then wept for the rest of the evening. I felt so loved. In one weekend God showed me that He had heard my cries and that yes, I could create and worship Him in this way. I was called to it. I didn't have to agree with fear of being called out for doing what I did for the pleasure of God.

This could have been Mary's excuse. I mean, think about the first time we meet her in the scriptures. She got called out for listening to Jesus by the one who should have understood her the best. You could imagine that she would be looking for permission to show such an extravagant display of worship. As we discussed earlier, I have a feeling the whole incident with Lazarus when her sister called her back to Jesus, helped get these sisters on the same page and to understand each other's gifts. Martha was now content and confident in her hospitality role. She was no longer comparing but taking her own beauty out of the box and serving extravagantly. Her gift was never in question when the Lord corrected her. He just needed to remind her of the beauty that was hers for the taking. The relationship with Him that was the source and center of her work. When she got in the right alignment, her work of hospitality became worship too. From this place Mary stepped out in boldness and humility to prophetically anoint her friend, King Jesus, with her most valuable possession. She didn't let herself get boxed in and therefore didn't let her gift sit on a shelf. She traded temporary satisfaction for what would speak volumes in eternity.

You see, I'm not just talking about the obvious here. Many times, we limit acts of beauty and worship to things that we deem to be in the creative artistic realm. But that is not how our God works. All of us were endowed with gifts and callings and the core purpose of all of them is to minister to our Lord. To bring glory to Him. He is looking for those who will love Him purely, giving back in joy and laughter all their favorite things. He is actively seeking according to John 4, ones who will worship Him in spirit and in truth. If He is seeking this type of authentic unboxed worship, then when you live and breathe and work in this way you are drawing His presence into whatever room you step into. You are breaking barriers by breaking open your alabaster box over and over, whatever that looks like. I hesitate to even give you more examples because I don't want even my own limited illustrations to box you in. You know what makes your heart beat. You know what you have been holding so dear to your heart, wondering if you can trust it out there in the world. You can remember the things you enjoyed as a child before rules and responsibilities shooed them away. You know what it is that you do that causes you to sense heaven open and the smile of the Lord all over you.

For me is writing. It means the most to me, words unlock so much. And sometimes I avoid it. It's too deep, too personal, sometimes painful to see my inner musings out there on display. But when I write, and I stay and dig in, I feel like my spirit has plugged into a power source. The Holy Spirit surges in me like a stream and words and images and prose and poetry and the prophetic flow out. And the ceiling above me gets thinner and thinner and I feel God peeking over. Smiling at the scribbles of His little girl. I'm not saying all my words make sense or are even good but when every part of me aligns with this fingerprint of worship that He gave me, my soul cries out. I'm there at His feet, pouring it out my love, knowing that the atmosphere of my family and future and friends are shifting bit by bit because of the fragrance that fills the room.

When we are positioned next to the Lord like this, He then overshadows us. The Holy Spirit broods over us like He did before creation, releasing more creativity and the supernatural in our lives. If Peter's shadow could heal then the shadow of the Lord brooding over us will bring a release of the creativity of the supernatural in our lives. We have the opportunity to choose to dwell, to remain, to rest in His shadow. This doesn't mean we are not doing anything. I can't control what He does in me and through me. But I can control what I choose to believe, what I choose to lay down, what I choose to decrease so He can increase in me. There is a response I am responsible for. He will do the rest.

We have been given a gift, we are sons and daughters that have been created for a purpose. Our purpose is to bring light, to bring glory to the Lord. To stand as His ambassadors in creation, declaring who He is and what He does. Jesus died on the cross to bring us salvation, to rescue us from the penalty of sin and bring us back into full relationship with the Father. All of this sounds great right? Really lofty and beautiful and romantic. But how many of you sometimes feel like those beautiful things are not the real world or at least your world? The intention for us was not to just talk about it or post beautiful pictures about it or set up some false image about it. We sometimes have this view and expectation of Christianity that is failing us because its incorrect. Many of you feel as if your expectations of Christianity have been too high so you need to lower them so that you won't get hurt, because you have been hurt by people and circumstances.

But I propose to you that your view of being in relationship with Christ is maybe too low, you have expected little to nothing maybe of your relationship and so therefore expect little to nothing of yourself. You've let circumstances tell you who God is and therefore who you ought to be. We've at times become like people of the past, making God into our image and because we have failed each other, because we are imperfect then God must be too. But this is so wrong. God is so perfect,

He is mighty, He is powerful, and He is so good! He loves you so much. He didn't just create you; He didn't just give you life. He didn't even just provide a way for your salvation. He provided you a way to work out your salvation, to live the new normal that He intended for you and that is through the Holy Spirit.

Holy Spirit is our gift to navigate this crazy world, to operate just like Jesus did, to do signs and wonders, to have a close friendship with the Father. You have a great calling on your life to change the world, your world, your atmosphere, with His presence. The enemy wants to dismantle everything about you so that you won't do as Jesus has called you to. He has come to kill steal and destroy and one of His favorite ways of doing so is for you to be afraid and let it hold you back.

Holy Spirit comes and brings many gifts, including a prayer language to help us pray the perfect will of God and get to know Him more intimately. He gives boldness and wisdom. He helps us get to know Jesus better. He searches out with us the mysteries of God, the things that the Lord wants us to dig and pursue, to ask and receive. He wants us to be curious and look beyond the boxes we have made for Him and see how He wants to move in our lives. But if the enemy can get us to agree with fear not only do we not step out in our calling, we a lot of times don't walk in step with the One who was sent to be with us.

What rooms need to be broken by your brokenness? What lids and ceilings need to be lifted off because of what you unbox in your life? Father God is looking for worship from authentic you. The platform doesn't matter, it's just a tool. In the midst of it will you engage with Him and why you were created? Break open the boxes. Give yourself permission to dream with Him again. To bubble over with your imaginative questions and pondering. Find that pathway to His heart through Jesus so that He can pour into you what you are meant to pour out.

This authentic worship becomes sticky lingering influence that leaves a residue not easily gotten rid of. Because it's concentrated and pure and valuable. It remains. It's so potent that it shifts history and gets shared in the circles of wonderers and wanderers, of servants and seekers for years into the future. It's the type of anointed worship that will bid the hungry to come and at times the unrepentant to run. It's a game changer. And it can come through you.

Go Deeper into Intimacy

How do we get our hearts in the right position if we feel like we have gotten out of alignment? Looking through scripture I would suggest that we linger. Linger in God's presence. Stay longer than expected as Joshua did in Exodus 33:11. It's my hope that all of us continually cultivate intimacy in our lives.

To find more resources that deal specifically with areas of Intimacy please visit: www.milkandhoneywomen.com/intimacy-1

PART THREE

RELEASING INFLUENCE

Part Three

"Come, all you who are thirsty,
come to the waters;
and you who have no money,
come, buy and eat!
Come, buy wine and milk
without money and without cost."
Isaiah 55:1 NIV

"Your lips drop sweetness as the honeycomb,
my bride; milk and honey are under your tongue.
The fragrance of your garments
is like the fragrance of Lebanon."
Song of Songs 4:11 NIV

The Vessel Poured out

Is there a more powerful story in the Bible of a woman in leadership than Deborah? She was the only woman listed among the judges in the Old Testament. One who operated in wisdom, boldness and authority. She daily dispensed words of revelation, prophecy and insight into the lives of the people. All this before she was positioned next to Barack in the battle of their generation. However the highlight of her story is not in her gifting and call but in how intertwined her story was with another woman. Someone hidden in the background, a woman who was not a leader to the nation, just a leader in her own home. Yet both of them were positioned to operate together and became beautiful illustrations of God releasing His promises in the land. They were vessels, made whole, filled up and ready to pour out what was needed to bring influence in and outside of the home.

Her Moment of Influence

Deborah & Jael
(Biblical Account found in Judges 4 & 5)

Her eyes scan the horizon before her. It is the quiet before the storm and she craves this time, this solitude. It is her refuge, this place within the waking of the sun. No other voices distract her from hearing the One who beckons her to come. It wasn't always easy hearing Him, filtering out the noise to know what was Him and what was her own nonsense. It wasn't always easy but was actually so simple. As simple as a position, a pure heart, leaned in ear, a receptive posture. Her worn calloused knees could tell the tale of thousands of mornings. Getting low, heart turned to worship, even if she never heard a sound.

Deborah sought time and time again because she knew that the Lord had spoken before. She had heard the stories of old, how He moved for her people in times of oppression and wandering. If He had done it then, surely, He could do it now. And if no one else would try to listen, she would. Were they not now in similar times? They were oppressed by a very real enemy. But the most significant enemies they faced were their own wandering hearts. A stubborn and complaining people. They were always reminded, tried for a season to remain but got distracted and drifted away.

So, she sat. She listened and eventually she was summoned. It started out small at first, lending wisdom to family, speaking encouragement to friends. But soon word spread, and her family found more and more people at their doorstep. People in need of answers, calling her words life giving and prophetic. Calling her a prophetess. She who had only longed to listen and now whose words at times came out like a roar. And so, with the covering of her husband and family she moved from her dwelling to a palm tree to dispense her prophetic wisdom. It gave space and availability and boundaries so that her household would be at peace even as she stepped out to judge a nation.

They came from near and far, searching out truth in a time of such confusion. She had not understood it at first. Why they came to her, why she had been called to this. But as the people came with their problems and as they left with eyes alight with hope and reassurance, she realized that more than a lack of safety, or food or deliverance the people lacked leaders. The nation was in need of authentic mothers and fathers that spoke the truth in the sweetness of true love and compassion. She found herself in tears at times as some women enveloped her in grateful embraces or when some men quietly wept as close as they culturally could to her feet. The land was devoid of lasting influence, everyone trapped in survival mode because of the constant onslaught of enemies.

It was at this place, in the soft light of early morning, she positioned herself in God's presence once again so she could be positioned to speak to His people. This morning was no different. She saw the first groups of people in the distance, the fear and threats hovering overhead. And it was this morning, before her day began, that she heard the words from the Father that would define her life and her legacy. There was one she would send for when this day was done and declare to Him the words of war and victory. She smiled to herself. For there was more to this adventure, someone else unknowingly positioned to flex her own powerful wings.

Milk & Honey: Known

There are moments that feel like death.

So, gripping, so present, the heart break so cruel and unrelenting.

I don't want to make light of those who do pass in the physical,

the horror and grief of those that we love

no longer opening their eyes on this side of eternity.

But in transition there is a death that happens, truly,

more than the palpable feelings and emotions.

You have died. Or at least the you that everyone saw you as.

The you that was constructed and nurtured

by your past season and environment.

The you that learned to respond and produce and create

within the box that the years had slowly,

steadily built around you.

The you that people saw and loved and knew.

But in transition, in the stepping into the new, that part dies.

Not that you were fake or hypocritical

or as if the last part wasn't even true.

But now that you are in the new you must come face to face

with the part of you that you never knew that well.

Another layer closer to the core.

More stripped off to expose authentic you

to His awesome presence.

To be exposed and naked, allowing Him to empower you

to feel no shame.

To embrace your raw talents, raw gifting, raw anointing.
The raw, the real, the things even in need of repentance...
the person and personality that He gave you
unhindered and unfettered by people's perception.
Free to grieve, to breathe, to be...surrendered and submitted
to the shaping of your clayful form by His gentle creative hand.
It feels like death.
And some days you are doubled over by the weight of it.
But you are bent over not in isolation or loneliness,
despite what the enemy of your soul would try to convince you.
You are being bent and stretched and formed over and over,
knead upon knead in the hand of your Father.
Cupped and cultivated intimately, His breath on you always.
Dying daily, moving from glory to glory,
being perfected into the image that He already sees
when He looks at you not dimly, but full.
Through the blood of His son Jesus.
Fully His. Fully loved. Fully alive.
Fully known.

Chapter Eleven: The Delight of the Desert

As I look throughout the Bible I see a similar theme over and over. The Lord takes His people through a desert or wilderness season before a time of great breakthrough and promise. This place always seems to be one of transition, of moving from one place to another. From one season to the next. It's the hinge that turns you towards the next phase in your journey, the "to" between the movements from glory to glory. There is no roadmap for how long this time takes. For some it may be 40 days and for others it seemed to take 40 years. The length of time determined by obedience or lack thereof. Or simply defined by the type of process the Lord is trusting you to walk out. None of us are immune from these seasons. And to be honest with you. I am so glad.

I don't willingly walk into those moments. Ha. I don't think any of us ever do. We would rather intentionally choose the periods of rest and refreshing. But I would dare say the deserts of life are a good thing and I am finding myself thankful for them. Thankful even in the moments when tears or grief over change may be more frequent than we ever thought possible. Contained within the wilderness wanderings can be the exact things that we are praying for, if we have the eyes to see it. If we keep our eyes on Jesus.

There was a time in my life that I felt a shift of the Lord leading me into what I call a wilderness season. I was in my early twenties and this theme kept coming up over and over in my life that year. I even wrote in my journal that I felt like God was bringing something significant my way in the fall of that year but before that time He was drawing me in closer to Him. It started with this verse found in Hosea 2:14.

"Therefore, I am now going to allure her; I will lead her into the wilderness and speak tenderly to her." (NIV)

Even though I felt the outward change, the feelings of drought and discomfort, He was inwardly positioning me to become more intimate and dependent on Him. He was using circumstances and the leading of the Holy Spirit to draw me away from the noise into a place where I could only focus on His voice.

During that season I would wake up in the middle of the night multiple times a week, turn on my lamp and read the Bible. The verses He led me to spoke of His love and compassion, everlasting and unrelenting. I read of oil, fragrance and anointing and then I stumbled across a verse that caught my breath and gave me a greater understanding of the season I was in.

"Who is that coming out of the wilderness, leaning on the one she loves?" Song of Songs 8:5 NIV.

I was overwhelmed with the implications and romance of this verse. In context, this is part of the words written by King Solomon to His bride. It was also a birds-eye view look at the story of the nation of Israel. Coming out of the wilderness in submission and dependence on the Lord. But in that moment the Holy Spirit was highlighting to me what it would look like when I came out of this season. I was learning dependence on Him. He was making an exchange with me. Teaching me in his gentle way, that I needed to lay down my independence, keeping my walls up, letting fear run my life. It was time to give up my control, so that I could lean on Him. He was more than able to lift me up and care for me. And after it was all said and done I would be a woman coming up out of the hard, broke, desolate, confusing, isolating places, leaning on the one I loved.

Amazingly enough, after this time I actually found myself with the opportunity to share with other women at my first conference speaking opportunity. The one that I mentioned early in this book. It was the significant breakthrough that came for me in the fall. I don't think I would have been positioned for that opportunity and had the words to pour out if it wasn't for the season where the Lord drew me in and drew me close.

Song of Songs 8:5 is such a beautiful verse on intimacy and dependence. I heard a minister recently saying that if God had a love language that His love language would be trust. For me, faith is big picture, that thing that we move and point our lives towards. But trust brings definition and makes all of our actions, thoughts, and beliefs intentional. Will we trust Him in the midst of what we need to have faith for?

The wilderness facilitates this type of wrestling. Laying down what we have used as our comfort and crutch for so long in order to grab a hold of the Lord as our strength and full dependence. To trust Him deeply. At first, this season may seem like scarcity and desolation. Truth be told we are not meant to dwell in this place for always. In fact, it was the Israelites disobedience that caused them to have to stay too long in the wilderness. Yet when it is God orchestrated, He sets us up to be able to rely completely on Him. And then the place that seems lacking begins to feel like abundance because all of us is grabbing a hold of all of Him. We can't lean on anything and anyone else. We have to look at Him as our source.

Many times, we perceive our season of wilderness as a prison sentence, but I think the Lord looks at it as a time to get closer to Him. In order for Him to be the source of our delight, just as we are the source of His. The apple of His eye. He makes promises in the desert, to you and I. Forming out of the ashes of our transition and past season something new and beautiful. A woman transformed by the personal and intimate love of God.

"See, I am doing a new thing! Now it springs up; do you not perceive it? I am making a way in the wilderness and streams in the wasteland."
Isaiah 43:19 NIV

Often, the new is hard to perceive within the context of the old. And unless you are detoxed from the old you can't see the new for what it is. You don't rejoice in where you are going or what the Lord is doing within you. This was the struggle of the Israelites. They couldn't fully embrace what the Lord was doing for them because they continued to look back at what they had been brought out from. The oppression of past seasons began to take on a rosy hue in light of the fear they agreed with in the face of potential freedom.

The desert has a way of detoxing you, getting the Egypt out of you that was hidden within the warmth of comfort and familiarity. It exposes the things that maybe you would not have dug out in another season. And these expeditions into your soul are necessary to redeem what happened then and to prepare you for whatever it is will come. If you desire to go too quickly through the process, you won't have what you need for the next mountain top or platform or opportunity. Even in the undoing that takes place in these moments, you are so safe and cherished and loved. God doesn't just love you *through* the process, He loves you *in* the process. All the messy, broken, raw parts of you that get to be rebuild and renewed in the safe space of desert places.

I think this is why so many in the Bible that had extended fasts actually went into the wilderness. It was a safe place for their detoxing. They could shut out all the noise without fear of reprisal and reprimand. Allowing themselves to stay hidden on the potter's wheel, for Him to mold and shape without exposing the forming parts before its time. Think of how close you are to the Lord in these moments. How proud He is of you even within your frailty and transparency, how close you are to once again being knit together in the womb, formed from the dust of the ground. This time is essential for your growth and for your depth with the Lord.

He wants to use these times to deepen what He has declared over you in order to maximize your influence and effectiveness. It was after the Lord spoke about Jesus during His baptism that He was led into the desert by Holy Spirit. And the enemy sought to test the very words the Lord declared. Instead of denying them, they were deepened in Jesus. It was after this time that Jesus called His disciples and started His earthly ministry. But this practice of being with the Lord continued even throughout His kingdom work. The Bible says that He often withdrew to lonely places. Not to be alone per say but to be alone with the Father. That is the key. When you know the Lord, wilderness seasons are not to be places of isolation but places where you are alone with the Lord.

You may feel like you are drowning in your hidden, transitional desert season but if you will keep your eyes on Jesus, be led by Holy Spirit and trust your Father you will realize that this season is only meant to deepen you. To get you in line with the deep wells of provision that are available for you so that when it's time you yourself will overflow with living water and His supernatural provision.

I find myself in a similar season now to that one of over ten years ago. But this time the Lord has led me, initially kicking and protesting, into a different type of wilderness. He has brought the physical shift into my life that has set me up to once again seek Him and His voice as I moved from a place of comfort and family to a completely different country. The landscape itself in certain areas can lend to a sense of barrenness and vastness but undeniable beauty. I imagine your own season may not be too far off if you are not in one right now. Transition can hit us through new jobs, new locations, new babies, babies leaving, relational change, loss of loved ones or other intentional or unintentional shifts. But in all of it I know that the Lord uses this time to allure you, to romance you from the place you are in to the place that He is. He works out all the details, taking care of things in the background so that you can be right where you need to be to take delight in Him. And for Him to show you how much He delights in you.

The heavens have been saturated with words and songs and teachings about who we are, about our identity. And rightly so because we never need to forget that a price was paid by Christ for us to be the children of God, He our Abba Father and us, co heirs with Christ. Now in this season of transition the message is turning to intimacy, abiding in Christ in order to be positioned for greater influence in whatever sphere we are sent to. We can't just lean on our public personas to sustain us. No, all of us are without excuse. All of us called to go deeper and further. To seek out not what improves our image but what forms the image of Christ within us. It's like I hear the shout in the spirit "Remember who you are, remember where to go and remember what to do!"

Even in grief there is a level of faith and trust that is released that can affect those around us. A dear mother in the faith just recently passed to be with the Lord after a yearlong battle with cancer. I even use the term battle loosely because in the midst of this infirmity her concern was not about herself but that she would be an influence for Christ and win as many people over to the Lord as she could. She wanted this wilderness season used for the Lord's glory. She did not choose for her life to be ended this way, but she made choices out of the overflow of a life that was rooted and grounded in the Lord. When we live our lives out of the overflow of that kind of abiding, we can't help but leak Christ even in times of extreme brokenness. Even what seems to be dying is used as seeds for what will soon live.

Really knowing what your season is and who is in your sphere of influence helps you make specific and intentional decisions for you and those around you. For this mother in the faith, her sphere of influence was her family and friends, the people who came to visit, the doctors and nurses and other patients around her. For me in this season it's not just the people we interact with in Iceland, the churches we help, or the people affected by our weekly radio program. For me more acutely in this season, it's my children. That is my main place of influence, where what I release should be the strongest and most potent. I know my actions will nurture them more than my words will. I want them to know that I value my relationship with the Lord, my relationship to their father and my relationship to them.

Out of that overflow of who you are in intimacy with the Lord, you can be anointed in what you do in influence. Because the enemy knows that, He doesn't always go after what you *do*. A lot of times He overemphasizes that part so that you lose sense of who you are. This is what happens many times to those with much influence, fame or opportunity that are not grounded in character and relationship. The enemy is not always trying to cut us off from our talents or our skills. He's not always trying to tell us to work less or stop putting forth so much effort.

Our accuser goes for the jugular. He goes for what matters most. He goes for our intimacy with the Lord. He knows that if we lose the connection with our Father, that what we do will eventually bury us, burn us out, dishearten and overwhelm us. He distracts us away from intimacy with Jesus and deceives us into putting more emphasis on the good things that we do rather than the GOD thing that we are supposed to focus on. He takes attention away from what should be our foundation, from what should be our core.

He causes us to step away and therefore, doubt, defy and deny what the Lord has declared over us. Sometimes we end up in trials and storms and wonder what in the world is going on. You're like, I just had this awesome encounter with the Lord, He declared things over me, He gave me dreams but now all Hell has broken loose. We end up operating almost opposite to what we know to be true. This is the enemy's intention. But we serve a God who can take any circumstance and turn it into a place where that declaration is actually deepened instead of denied. The desert and wilderness spaces turn into the places where we see the new thing springing up, the streams flowing and delight in the Lord that we thought we may never experience again.

One of the best illustrations of this is in the story of the prophet Elijah found in the Bible. You can read more in 1 Kings 18 & 19. But the essence is that Elijah had a great victory against the evil King & Queen of Israel, Ahab and Jezebel, and all of their false prophets. Listen. You would be feeling the victory too if the Lord brought fire down from the sky among the other amazing things he did in this story. Not to mention Elijah totally destroying hundreds of false prophets. Yet when Jezebel, one woman, issued a threat to his life, he ran like the wind and gave in to fear and discouragement. In the beginning of this story he was confident in his place as the seemingly only prophet totally dependent on God. But now in vs 10 he is insecure in his place as the only prophet and questioning the Lord. Why? Because the enemy was after what was declared. But the Lord drew Elijah in deeper into the wilderness to meet him and restore him. He invited Elijah to encounter His presence. In the most intimate and special way. In a whisper. Sometimes the best place to hear that whisper is in the quiet, lonely, hidden places of the wilderness. In those places you cultivate something sweet between you and the Lord that will never disappoint. It's something that when poured out, can bring life to the barren places around you, anointing that breaks the strongholds of those within your sphere of influence.

The Lord has declared something over you. Yes, its plan and visions and dreams but first and forever it is that you belong to Him. You are His daughter. You have been bought with a price; you have been born into a new family. We have to be on guard against any denial or defiance of our divine sonship (being sons and daughters of God), so that we won't be distracted out of the intimacy that leads to lasting influence. You are being positioned to release milk and honey that nourishes and propels others into their more. You see, milk and honey were what was promised in the wilderness. This was the land the Lord said He was taking the people of Israel into. A land flowing with it. A land teeming with the abundance of supernatural provision and nourishment. And as we will see even more clearly, this provision overflowed in the actions of two different women.

Release

1. When was the last time you felt like you were in a desert/wilderness season, if you are not in one now?

2. Did you find it was sweet time of intimacy with the Lord? Why or why not?

3. If you could look back or look within (depending on where you see yourself) what treasures did/does the Lord have for you? How do they relate to where you are now?

4. What declarations is the Lord deepening in you even now?

Chapter Twelve: The Cost of Comparison

There is so much strength and anointing that flows when the Body of Christ works together in unity. This is so powerfully evident in the story of Deborah and Jael. They didn't have to take personality or gifting assessments to determine how they fit together in the body. Don't get me wrong. These tools are wonderful resources that help communities, churches and groups operate efficiently and respectfully towards each other. Deborah and Jael operated from the position and place they were in for the victory of the nation, different though they were. Their actions set them up to be living illustrations of God's promise in the promised land.

Let's take a quick look at what God's promise of milk and honey symbolized. Milk was most likely obtained from domestic goats back in Biblical times. Milk in the Bible represents provision, life, sustenance, basic food, and according to one article "milk contains fat and fat represents the highest form of human love."[1] It's easy to picture this when you think of a mother nursing an infant. A position of tenderness and love as the infant receives nourishment in a mother's arms. Interestingly, goat milk more closely represents human milk than cow's milk does. Some of you may consider this picture and have second thoughts about what I am encouraging us to see released into the land. There is nothing hyper maternal or even sexual in what I'm sharing. But

I do want you to see how specific the Lord is in what He promised. He wants His people to enter into a place where all their basic, foundational, spiritual needs are met and where they experience how tenderly loved they are.

Honey on the other hand represented the sweet nectar of fruit or more frequently what was produced by wild bees back in Biblical times. It was obviously used as a sweetener for foods and drink, but it also has medicinal and preserving properties. It is rich in antioxidants, can help lower blood pressure, improve cholesterol, and can even help with the healing process of burns and wounds.[2] If you think about the physical benefits of these two substances, you begin to get an idea of how powerful of a representation they are. When milk and honey are flowing it implies that there are fertile and plentiful conditions in the land and access to water. Think about that. The milk and honey we release indicate we are connected to a source of sustenance that will never run dry. We can enter this place and operate in these ways as believers by what Jesus accomplished through the cross and His resurrection.

The momentum that arises from our agreement with Jesus and each other brings great impact. We see it in gatherings, movements, calls of prayer and fasting, corporate worship, generous giving, missionaries in various fields. But as methods and messengers get put more on public display, we must guard ourselves against a weapon that the enemy uses so often to derail us off of our own post on the wall. This weapon is the one of comparison. The type of comparison that doesn't make us better but that leads us away from God's heart and intention for us. If you consider milk and honey, they are two totally different liquids. Yet they are powerful and effective in their own ways and even more so when they are used together.

We all know and have heard the words encouraging us to not compare ourselves to others, to see our own worth and be united in sisterhood. We hear it all the time, but do we really believe it and walk out that belief? There is a real agenda in the lie of the enemy that tells us we must be exactly like our sister in Christ. It's not only the opportunity for insecurity and self-doubt to grow, but also shows itself at times in a lack of desire to even move forward. How many times have you looked at someone's successful ministry or event or business and instead of excitement, felt resentful that you were not in that place in your own life? Especially when something similar you were doing didn't work out so well. Or maybe it's someone's family that you see on social media or social gatherings. Everyone seems more beautiful and more well-behaved and it was all you could do to make sure your children brushed their teeth this morning. Ok?! All these become mirrors that begin to surround us with reflections of the outward perspective of people's lives without any looks at the inner workings.

When you allow someone else to be your mirror versus the Word of God, you have placed that person as your standard and your limitation. Someone else's success (or even failure) becomes our ceiling and the lion share of opportunity. Therefore, you can move no further and can dream no higher. How real this becomes even as we brainstorm and put vision to what God has placed on our lives. If we are not careful, we will allow other's assessments to shift us away from our partnership with God. Instead of producing what the Lord has intended for us to, because of our comparison, we assume that someone else's call is a denial of our own. You may have been told the market is saturated and has no need of what you bring to the table. It is true that this can be a reality that we have to deal with when it comes to putting our gifts and creativity, business ideas and products out in the open. But in the Kingdom of God, nothing that we do out of our abiding with the Lord is ever wasted or in vain. And there is definitely a place for what the Lord has placed in you. It's not about the notoriety or fame that may come with it. It's about making Jesus famous upon the earth.

We need to gain understanding and see this demonic parasite of comparison for what it is. When we come into agreement with comparison, we may abort our own dreams even before they have the chance to flourish! They won't even have the chance to sprout. We snatch our seeds away because of our unbelief and don't feel like it's even worth it to try to risk, or to hope. The enemy doesn't even have to steal, kill and destroy our dreams because comparison does it for us. More faith is put in the abilities of someone else to trump our gifts than in the One who gave us the gifts in the first place. The One who created us for this very season and a specific hour. We stand as Moses did in front of the burning bush, constantly pointing the finger at ourselves; constantly demeaning the work of our Creator. All because we can't speak as fluently as our sister, or sing as well, or look as pretty or dress as nice or have the right amount of money, or the right filters on Instagram or her contacts or her platform.

This is the unfortunate state the church finds itself in because everything is on such hyper display. Consider what Paul says in 2 Corinthians 10:12-13:

> **"But when they measure themselves by one another and compare themselves with one another, they are without understanding. But we will not boast beyond limits, but will boast only with regard to the area of influence God assigned to us, to reach even to you." (ESV)**

There is a specific area of influence that God has assigned all of us to. It is the post on the wall that we are meant to occupy and steward well. But we also sell ourselves short thinking that God wants our influence alone. No sister, He wants our obedience, He wants our love. He wants us to look in the mirror He places in front of us, though our view be partially hidden and trust that He sees and knows us fully. And in knowing us, in partnering with us, He places seeds and dreams and vision and hope in us that need the soil of our uniquely surrendered lives to flourish. This is the understanding we gain when we do not compare but seek out the counsel of the Holy Spirit. When we compare ourselves to one another we rob ourselves of the opportunity to dream authentically. We conjure up an image that is counterfeit and so far from what the Lord wants to manifest in our lives. We deceive ourselves into thinking that there is no place for us. We deceive *ourselves*. Once again, the sly sinister lies of the enemy are listened to. We place the forbidden fruit in our own mouths, disregarding what Heaven has to say over us. Dear sister, heaven has much to declare over you.

I made a decision at one time to help stem the tide of doubt and insecurity that was bombarding me. I decided to do my best to get off social media for one month. To position myself to hear His whispers again instead of my own counterfeit longings to see what others were shouting. I thought I was comforting myself with viewing a multitude of posts because I was feeling homesick and wanted to stay connected with my family and friends back in the States. And they were all good, fun, and even inspiring things. But I didn't realize how much it was costing me. I enjoyed getting to see the things I was missing but slowly I could feel the fear of man creeping back up in my life. It was not social media any more for me, but a social comparer. Setting a skewed mirror in front of my eyes that didn't necessarily give me something to attain to but distorted my motivation and dampened my passion. What was I doing just for eyes to see? And what was I *not* doing because it seemed like it wouldn't matter?

Comparison is truly a thief of joy. It is such a simply profound statement that many of us mistakenly think it's in the Bible, but it actually is a quote from Theodore Roosevelt. He definitely did not live in a time where you could have the published lives of millions of people at your fingertips. If his words were true for his time, how much more do they apply now? We have the ability to access the accomplishments of others in an instant. We are able to take in the highlight reels of those we admire without seeing what they did to count the cost. We don't see the years of preparation, of tending sheep, of outright rejection that they may have gone through. We compare our hidden moments to their public influence and so diminish the place where we are now.

Comparison is one of the greatest tools the enemy uses to handicap the Body of Christ. We as a church end up walking with a limp not just because of sin or foolish choices but because some decide that their role isn't good enough, isn't as important as others. So considering the illustration of the body, it's as if the toe bows out, the little fingers decline to engage, maybe one kidney says, nah, I'm not needed. And soon we have a body of self-inflicted harm, deciding to sit out when they were always called out to be a part of the fullness of God's kingdom. A full body, a whole Bride has always been His intention.

We desire to do something that will honor God but does our comparison bring Him glory? Do we not diminish His work, His creativity when we look with longing at someone else's life? There are such things as inspiration and challenge and motivation. Iron sharpening iron is necessary for our spiritual accountability and growth. Paul himself said follow me as I follow Christ; Christ being the main focal point of discipleship.   And there are moments we may observe the life of someone else and see that they have something that we are hungry for. We hope that we stir up this kind of hunger in those that do not know Christ. There is a place for that type of contrast that comes out of discipleship, transparency, humility and a servant's heart. And it should not lead to shame but bring conviction and a desire for Christ-like change. The comparison I speak of is not that. It is a cultivator of envy, of jealousy, of apathy, of jadedness, of cynicism, of bitterness, of depression. No wonder the Lord told us not to covet. When we open that door, we allow ourselves to take steps towards something that never belonged to us, to possible temptation and sin that could hinder God's purposes flowing through us.

This is why I believe it was necessary for Jesus to stop Martha in her tracks when she called out her sister and compared what she was doing with what her sister was engaging in. He gave her the opportunity to see her question for what it was, an act of envy and resentment that would cost her much more if she continued in that direction. It would open the door to bitterness in her life that would not allow the glory of God to flow through. Her exact response in this scene is not recorded in scripture but we know that she eventually made the right choice, just like her sister did. As we discussed in earlier chapters, she was the one who later approached Jesus in bold faith after her brother Lazarus died. She knew that if Jesus had been there, her brother Lazarus would not have passed. It could have been a moment of major rejection and resentment. But she did not linger there; in the next breath she declares that Jesus can do the impossible. She came into agreement with Christ and saw her sister reconnected and her brother resurrected. You see, the cost is so much greater than we can imagine if we let comparison lead us. There are people strategically placed in the path of your authentic call. They wait on your obedience to encounter the life giving presence of Jesus that you bring.

Holy Spirit wants to break comparison off your life so that instead of moving from side to side swayed by the crowd, you are moving forward with focused, faith fueled steps towards Jesus. At a certain point that dear daughter in the crowd had to decide to stop comparing what she did not have so that she could grab hold of what she needed. She came into agreement with who Jesus was instead of what circumstances dictated to her. Therefore, she was able to grab hold of her healing and loose her title of being forgotten, unclean and unhealed. She stirred up hope that she could be healed, and Jesus made her whole. Hope in Christ is a great motivator and silencer of comparison. When we decide to hope, we part the crush of the crowd and grab a hold of what the Lord has for *us*. In an environment clogged with the search for rights and equality, we need to manifest what it means to be daughters of God. Daughters seek not after the things that would bring them simple equality with others, but they are hungry for EVERYTHING that God their Father has for them.

If you are praying for just what your sister has you miss out on what God holds in His hand for *you*. This is one of the biggest lessons my husband and I teach our children. Snack time seems to always lead to competition and they complain over not having exactly what their sibling has. We want to make sure that they understand that there are times we want to bless them specifically and individually and that if they settle for just getting the same, they may miss the abundance we have for them. As a woman I don't just want equality with a man. It is foolish to desire equality with someone that is completely different from me and camp out there. I want what God wants for me. I want the freedom and rights and healing and confidence and deliverance and abundance and gifts and call that He has determined for me to have.

We must turn our eyes from the sin of coveting and seek what has been promised for each of us. I remind you friend that Jesus is the mirror into which we are to look. He is the one we are to model ourselves after. Your mirror is not your sister, your mirror is your Savior. He wants us to reflect Him, not the world around us. He is the one who is the Word. Was at the beginning and ever will be. Sharp and active, piercing the lies to bring you to the truth of who you are. Comparing ourselves to Him will not bring shame but true repentance, restoration and change. He is the light by which everything else dulls and fades. Through His eyes we see what really matters regardless of what people say or do. He is the one who sees you clearly, calls you by name and catapults you into the call that can't be determined by anyone else and what they are doing.

Aren't you glad that Deborah and Jael did not operate in comparison or even competition but instead walked in celebration! I love the song of Deborah found in Judges 5 because she did not even diminish herself when she sang Jael's praises and celebrated the victory that came through another woman's hands. She was a woman fully confident in her gifting and position and knew that the victory of a sister did not mean that the light dimmed on her any less. We are never shadowed by anyone. It is only the shadow of our Father's wings that we willingly step under in humility so that as He surrounds us, it is *His* presence that overcomes in each and every circumstance.

Release

1. What in your life do you need to turn your eyes away from in order to break agreement with comparison? As you do, make sure to turn your eyes to Jesus through the Word and worship.

2. Is there another person in your life that you can celebrate today? Send a note or a message or a gift that will support what they are doing.

Milk & Honey: Content

Sometimes I am content.

I stand brewing coffee thankful for the grounds that are being

filtered through

and the ground covered by toys strewn across,

bits and pieces under my feet.

Bits and pieces of noise and melody

filtering in from the overflow of chaotic joy

that is my child or children,

the combination of them intoxicating and brash.

They draw me in to a moment

where I don't wish for it to be different,

for it to always remain.

Lazy days and the sounds of their footsteps adventuring,

their tongues imagining

as they try to keep up with the wilds

that are their minds of childhood.

I breathe in deep, taking this eternal moment into my chest.

Letting it expand my lungs with hope and thankfulness,

pushing out the desire to be known by anyone else.

If only God allows for me to be known by them

and for Him to be seen in all that they glean from me.

Their coffee craving mother,

who most days has to be intentional

about pushing down frustration,

answering with a gentle tongue and just simply playing.

Many times, I am restless but desiring for constant peace

and consistency and simplicity

to overtake my wandering heart and settle me

from looking for tomorrow,

for the future,

for that which is ever before my eyes,

but currently out of my grasp.

But I am growing.

As all of us are.

Moving from the glory of past seasons to the glory of another.

Never forgetting the beauty and significance

of the place that is in between.

However long the distance.

So sometimes I am content and I engage in eternal moments.

Breathing in the air of the present,

taking in the luminosity of little eyes,

sipping on thankfulness as liquid in my mug.

Chapter Thirteen: The Significance of your Season

It may have become a cliché term these days, but I say it here because it is necessary for us to grasp as women who follow Jesus. We need to reclaim the narrative. You know the one. Or the many depending on how you look at it. As women we are often pressured to come into agreement with a very broad view of what it should mean to be a woman in modern society. Or on the other end of our spectrum, we are told to come into agreement into a very narrow view of Biblical Womanhood. We look at it with just one perspective, one lens and let that set the standard for all women. That our only place is in the home, or that we have to have a full time career to have any influence. Or many of us, maybe because of hurt, disappointment or cultural influence, think that the Bible is against women and holds them down. These could not be farther from the truth.

Biblical womanhood is as varied as our fingerprints. Biblical women who God used were servants, queens, concubines, ex-prostitutes and former demoniacs. They were women who were married five times or never at all. They were little girls and pregnant teens. They were stay at home moms and moms who went to work. They were prophets and businesswomen, women with issues and women with none. They were orphans and widows, over-workers and those who worshipped extravagantly. We need to stop pointing the finger of comparison and remember that we are called the Body of Christ, one that has many different parts and functions. We need to remember as we look in the mirror that our own bodies are not just the fingers and eyes and arms and legs and breasts and toes. But it's also our organs, our bones, our blood, our cells that make us who we are. The hidden parts do so much for the body that we can't even comprehend. We need to speak life and empowerment over each other and place a demand on the anointing on our sisters to be who they were created to be.

Stop the condemnation of your humble, hidden season or lifetime if God says it so. Don't look at the roles you don't understand as just another example of being less than or looked down on. Look at yourself the way God sees you and move the ground that He's called you to move, to stir and sow seed into. Maybe the place you are in now is because He needs you at the ground to remove the roots at your fingertips. To feel the vibrations and sounds of generations and break off the curses that have hindered fruitfulness. Maybe He is calling you to dig deep because your arms have been equipped for digging, for destroying, for driving tent pegs into the heads of generational enemies. No, don't despise your season. For maybe you are not seen but I tell you, you wield greater influence when you engage in what is unseen where you are.

This perspective does not downplay the roles of outward influence and favor. But what it should do for all of us is move us to seek an inner position of humility and confidence. So that if and when the Lord brings you out in the open for public influence, you have the character and stability, the relationship and intimacy to move and sway with God and not be swayed by others or their opinions.

Consider the deacons who were called to serve in the book of Acts. Stephen, the first Christian martyr was among them. These weren't just men who were called to serve tables and take care of the needs no one else had the time to. They were men who knew Jesus. They may have spent time hidden in shadows for a season but were now placed in a position of public influence. And think about it. That influence was serving and giving and in the midst of that they moved in power and authority. When you allow fear of man to distract you and get you off target you will miss the intention of Jesus putting you in a specific position. The purpose for where He's placed you.

Do you know how significant you are and the significance of the season you are in now? No matter how unflattering and unglamorous it seems? But what will you do with it? Will you use the moments contained within your specific season to be His? Will you use your voice to call women and men and children to Him? We bring people to where we are. If you are not with Him where or who are you calling them to?

Take an honest look at your situation to get a grasp of your season. Heighten your awareness to take in the things you may have been missing in the quest for more. Not just what is supposed to be done, but where are you now? I think too many times we focus on the process we are in or the specific season of our lives and consider it merely the means to the next big thing. But if we fail to live fully in the current moment, we may miss the big thing that is forming within the "now" places of our lives. So take a look around. Sniff the air. Observe the change in the environment. Adjust your wardrobe accordingly. Isn't this what we do when the seasons physically change? At least for those of you who experience four distinct seasons. Here in Iceland, the seasons barely ever get as warm as I would like and sometimes surprise me with the diversity in cold temperature and type in a day.

We know when things are shifting and we know when we find ourselves somewhere totally different from where we were a month, or a year ago. Do you feel it? And do you hear His whisper, beckoning you to come? To not disengage but to grab hold of the momentous occasions that are right under your nose? Out of this overflow of your specific season you will discover the significance of it. And the steps you are to take that take ground, even when you don't think they do.

That is how sensitive we need to be to the Holy Spirit. Especially when it comes to how we engage with others. We need to ask, Lord, what is needed here? Do I need to serve, do, pray, comfort, be silent, or is this a moment that I'm serving you by sitting with you and listening? What needs to be released in this moment? In the story we read of in Judges 4 and 5, Deborah was aware of what needed to be released in her moments. From her place as a judge she spoke in authority and boldness to Barak, the commander of Israel's army. She told him the word the Lord spoke to her, calling him to go fight the enemy. And then after Barak's response, asking if Deborah would go with him, she spoke prophetically. A word that seemed strange or almost ambitious. She told Barak that she would go with him but because of the course he was taking the honor will not be his, but that the Lord would deliver Sisera (the general of the enemy's army) into the hands of a woman.

Instinctively we think Deborah is referring to herself. Predicting that now the honor would be hers when she rode into battle with Barak. But when you continue to read the story in Judges 4, we see the scene change. It goes to the home of a man named Heber and his family. Going about their normal business and day to day affairs. Jael doing what other women did during those times, bustling in and out of her tent, performing her normal daily chores and duties. Arms strengthened by holding children, kneading bread, looking after herds and setting up tents. Little did she know how significant her insignificant acts would become for the people of Israel. Deborah's role mattered greatly for the nation. But so did Jael's. More than she realized. And when Deborah spoke to Barak, she positioned herself for greater influence and at the same time called out another sister to be positioned for the same.

We truly are significant. But we don't always see it that way for a myriad of reasons.

Sometimes we let our mistakes disqualify us from our God dream but it's even in those instances that God wants to bring restoration and hope. Or maybe we willingly choose the wrong direction because we think that it doesn't matter what we do or at least hope it doesn't. But all throughout the Bible I see the significance of just one person played out over and over. I think of Miriam and of Achan. I think of Rahab and of Boaz. About how God used Miriam to rescue the baby who would be the deliverer of the Hebrew nation (Exodus 2) and then much later how God stopped an entire Israelite camp from moving forward to allow Miriam to be disciplined and restored (Numbers 12). Of how Achan underestimated how important his actions were to the conquering of the promised land. Thinking that the pressure was all on the leaders and not on him (Joshua 7). Of how Rahab's desire for God despite her past caused a way of rescue to be made for her and her family (Joshua 2). Or of how, even though he waited long, Boaz's integrity and generosity caused him to be pinpointed by God as a husband for Ruth and the great-grandfather of a king.

These accounts may not all seem like typical feel good stories. I don't think we want to think of ourselves of being significant in some of those negative ways, but we need to be aware of the sobering reality of what can come when we don't know who we are. Of what can take place when we don't choose to be with Jesus. Releasing influence that doesn't glorify Him but instead points away from Him. It's hard to hear some of these things but the Bible is clear about all the situations and scenarios that can take place from the actions of one. Why would we be any different?

Significance is in your DNA, in the way God formed you. And to know the you that He formed, you have to know Him. It is now, where you are in your sphere of influence, that you play a significant part. Yet there is also a bigger picture you are a piece of. And we may never know the implications of our actions until we can see the big picture from heaven. We are the ones blessed to see the lives and actions of the people in the Bible from our current perspective, but most of them had no idea what God would do through their lives.

Understanding their individual significance allowed Deborah and Jael to both operate in ways that brought victory to the nation of Israel. They didn't have to work for unity in this fight because the Holy Spirit caused that to happen out of the overflow of them engaging in their season and being obedient to His leading. He used those seeds to create an ending that was beautiful and impactful. A woman operating publicly within her gifts was able to call out the people to battle. And her words prophetically set the stage for a woman working full time at home to put the seal on the victory by destroying the enemy that entered her own household.

When we begin to call out our sisters in encouragement, affirmation and empowerment, we are partnering with the Holy Spirit to see all of His provision and dreams for us get released. There is such strength in this type of sisterhood. This is why we need you to be whole and to cultivate intimacy with Jesus. In doing so there is a part of the Body of Christ and then ministry of Christ to the earth that you fulfill. And when this happens, in our unity we release the milk and honey that the Lord promised would flow in the place He is bringing His people to.

Release

In a season that I don't fully understand, hold me close, tuck me in, make me yours over and over again. As the waves and breakers sweep over me, speak to my heart in the deep. Speak to my heart with the depth of words that formed the mountains underneath my feet. Speak to me in the deep. The crevices of rock that you place me in, while your glory surrounds without and within.

1. If you could give a name to it, what season do you feel like you are in right now?

2. What are the significant things about this season?

3. In what ways do you see that you are being uniquely positioned to bring influence?

4. What are 3 tangible things you can do this week (no matter how small) to release that influence?

Chapter Fourteen: Fighting the Familiar

I remember when everyone was becoming more and more aware of the prevalence of sex trafficking many years ago. I was in my early twenties and feeling so burdened for the plight of children and women in places I could not even imagine. I wanted a way to combat that darkness and make impact. But what I wanted to do seemed like just a drop in the bucket of the problem. This was during the time before I was married, when I was walking out a journey of singleness, purity of heart and focus in my bodily temple. And one day the Holy Spirit downloaded some things to me. The Holy Spirit began to speak to me about authority in the spirit and how powerful our prayers are, even when we are not physically close to a situation. He also told me that I could not fight something that had a hold of me. I could not battle something that had already defeated me on the inside.

It was then that He reaffirmed my choices and empowered me to continue to walk pure before Him. That I could stand in solidarity with my sisters by choosing not to give my body before I was in the covenant of marriage. And therefore speak deliverance and rescue and redemption over those who didn't have a choice in how their bodies were being used. I realized all those years ago how significant each individual person was in the Body of Christ.

Am I saying that it is our promiscuity and lax in sexual purity that has caused thousands of people to be caught up in the slave trade? Not necessarily. But what I am saying is that you, even you who think you can go unnoticed, that you do matter. You may see yourself as just the callous or mole or freckle in the body of Christ, but He sees you as such an integral part. So needed in fact that He desires you to be completely whole. And He doesn't want you to willingly walk into what He has called you to resist. Even if you have come into agreement with lifestyles that are contrary to His Word and His heart for you, you are not above redemption. It's as simple as repentance and surrender, leaning into the one who is as close as your very next breath, ever ready to reposition you.

Remember that beautiful verse in Hosea 2 that was shared in Chapter 11? If you continue with that verse you will read this:

> **"There I will give her back her vineyards, and will make the Valley of Achor a door of hope. There she will respond as in the days of her youth, as in the day she came up out of Egypt." Hosea 2:15 NIV**

At first glance you may be moved by the symbolism of it. It has beautiful imagery. But digging deeper there is something more redemptive and poignant. Remember Achan and his sin in the book of Joshua? Because he disobeyed the command of the Lord and took from Jericho what he should not have, his whole family was destroyed. Remember, his sin did not just affect his family. It caused the whole nation of Israel to lose what should have been an easy battle against the next town after Jericho.

This Valley of Achor is where Achan and his family were destroyed and represented a major defeat not just in a physical battle but in a spiritual one for the people of Israel. But do you see what this verse is saying? The Lord was going to take that place of disobedience and defeat and destruction and turn it into a door of hope. It would lead the way to a place of worship, abundance and relationship.

We can see how one person's choice in their inner life, in the privacy of their home can determine the defeat or deliverance of a nation. Inner integrity and alignment are crucial in order to be solution bringers. I don't think Jael realized every time she built up and tore down her tent that she held the solution to Israel's victory in her hands. Her arms were tested and well worn, faithful in her daily chores and routine. But the tent peg was only a tool, one of many she had at her disposal. The significant part of her story is that she made the choice to let each moment matter. She decided to make a move and destroy what was trying to destroy the people of Israel. She made a choice that Achan did not.

This is the beautiful part of Jael's role in this story. Her act of killing the familiar had generational impact. The battle was indeed turning. The Israelites collectively were defeating the Midianites through the efforts of the warriors led by Deborah and Barak. But it was Jael who brought the closure. She was the one that ensured the evil of this man would not continue for another day. He would not be able to wreak havoc for the children and children's children of Israel. Maybe something would come from someplace else but nothing that was under her watch would be allowed to remain.

Consider this. Jael did not go out looking for a battle to fight. She wasn't looking to be placed in a position where she would receive a word like Deborah did or to be asked to be a part of the physical battle. She wasn't in someone else's home trying to fight battles with them or for them. It definitely is a wonderful thing to crave spiritual gifts from God and this type of desire is not the same as coveting or comparison like we talked about before. It is about asking the Lord to give you ALL that He has for you. And it's important for us to come along side people in compassion and agreement when they are dealing with situations in their lives. But I don't want us to make the mistake of searching out battles to fight if we have not dealt with similar strongholds in our own lives. Wasn't it Jesus himself that said in Matthew 7:3-5:

"And why worry about a speck in your friend's eye when you have a log in your own? How can you

think of saying to your friend, 'Let me help you get rid of that speck in your eye,' when you can't see past the log in your own eye? Hypocrite! First get rid of the log in your own eye; then you will see well enough to deal with the speck in your friend's eye." NLT

Ouch! Aren't you so glad that at the beginning of this book we talked about the sweetness of Jesus, even during times of correction? You may read this and be taken aback by Jesus calling anyone a hypocrite, but He was not interested in glazing over this concept. In His absolute love He wants us to make sure that we are healed and whole. And what Jael did to Sisera takes it a step further. He is asking us to have integrity in our inner life, to destroy the things that are strongholds for us, for our families, for the generations after us. If we want the clarity to flow with supernatural milk and honey, we need to be real with ourselves and deal with the enemies that pop up in our sphere of influence.

And friend don't make it too complicated. Don't remove yourself from peace by striving to dig out every hidden place of your heart all at one time. It's hard to remain at peace inwardly if you are in constant worry and fear that you are not good enough because of x, y and z. If there are things that begin to pop in your head even now, they are probably obvious enemies that God is telling you to take out immediately. Deal with them and move on. And from there as you move out of the overflow of your identity and intimacy with the Lord, He will begin to reveal things to you to deal with in His way and in His timing. We need to search our hearts through the lens of the Holy Spirit. In His wisdom He knows just what to highlight and what to pinpoint in the areas that we steward. In His perfect timing.

The hardest part of the first few months of my family's move to Iceland wasn't the culture shock, or the homesickness or getting acclimated to the weather. It was the process of detox the Lord took me on. Similar to what the Lord revealed to me while I was on maternity leave with my 2nd child,[1] Holy Spirit was bringing so many things to the surface. I didn't see them while I was in the midst of my season working full time at the church, moving, selling a house, buying a house, saying yes to our move to Iceland, preparing for the move, etc. But as things quieted and I had time to get on the floor with my infant son and gaze out over the beautiful mountains surrounding our apartment, I was able to hear His still sweet voice. And I didn't always like it, but I had the space to grieve the areas that I had grieved Him.

I was able to see His perspective on areas of my personality that were not always good, or helpful or submitted. I was able to surrender the pieces of my heart that were still broken from hurt and disappointment. He was detoxing me and uncovering the hidden places in my life that needed to be destroyed. This didn't happen during the previous season where I honestly did not have the capacity to do anything beyond the daily steps of obedience and planning. I was maxed out with just doing what needed to be done to move forward. The Lord was so sweet to reveal things to me in the timing that I needed and in ways that would not leave me in shame and regret but would catapult me to His feet and allow me to reposition myself before Him in surrender and repentance.

And now with more clarity I find myself able to pray with more compassion over others and the areas I am stewarding. I am able to look at my children and see the areas that the enemy may try to use against them. It gives me insight into how I can love them and pray for them specifically. It's putting the tent peg into the temples of those enemies that were not just affecting me but were poised to wreak havoc on my family in the future.

Holy Spirit is not interested in bombarding you with all the ways you need deliverance, healing, mindset shift, perspective altered, brain-washed, habits changed in one fell swoop. I don't think any of us would be able to survive that type of absolute change. Even when people have the most powerful Damascus road experiences, there is still growth that takes place in their lives afterwards. It doesn't change the promise and our standing in Christ. It doesn't alter the words of Jesus when He declared "It is finished" from the cross. It just means that we are truly people that are saved and going through the process of sanctification. A people moving from glory to glory, listening to His voice, walking in the way He leads. Consider this verse:

> **"I will send the hornet ahead of you to drive the Hivites, Canaanites and Hittites out of your way. But I will not drive them out in a single year, because the land would become desolate and the wild animals too numerous for you. Little by little I will drive them out before you, until you have increased enough to take possession of the land." Exodus 23:28-30 NIV**

From this verse we see that the Lord desires to increase your capacity in a way that is beneficial to you and whatever it is that He has called you to do. As we are faithful to obey Him and move with Him, He will do the driving out and destroying. And He won't ask us to fight in a battle that we are unequipped to fight. It may still look impossible and daunting but when we look to Jesus, we will see that He's given us exactly what is needed to fight whatever battle is placed before us. He trains your hands for war as you are faithful to your time with Him, your gifts and talents, your training and skill. Every single moment is an opportunity for worship, even the mundane work that fills our daily lives. That worship becomes the soundtrack to a life of faith and victory. It becomes the theme song of a woman who knows *who she is, where to go and then what to do*. It's hard to see it that way when the laundry never ceases, the phone never stops, the noise never dies down, the child doesn't seem to want to get potty trained, or your relationship status doesn't change. It's a fight to find the significance in the ordinary tasks. Yet it was the ordinary task that actually trained Jael's hands and arms for her most powerful act.

There was strength in her limbs. She had perfected the art of driving down tent pegs for her nomadic family as they moved from place to place. This was true of most people of that area and in Israel. Her family undoubtedly had flocks of sheep and goats and maybe other animals that they herded and cared for. Even if she had a multitude of servants it would be her role to oversee the daily milking of those goats for milk to drink and make into cheese. Her faithfulness to these chores in this season fully equipped her to fight the familiar enemy that appeared at her doorstep. I don't think she ever considered that these acts would lead to anyone's demise, much less Sisera. Her family was supposed to be a neutral party. They were friendly to both the Israelites and Midianites. And truthfully, we don't know the nature of the relationship between King Jabin, his general and Heber's family. But in this moment Jael made the choice to no longer be neutral. She couldn't waver between two places any longer and hold back because of fear. Sometimes the familiar things in our lives are the hardest to let go of. We fear the impact more than the freedom that could come.

The Bible doesn't tell us what happens after this battle besides the land being at rest for another generation. We don't know if Jael becomes well known. If people continued singing her praises and wrote more songs about her. If she found a place of honor among Israel's elite and is invited to "all the things". We don't know if her followers increased on social media and if she was invited to share her testimony at multiple venues. If she and Deborah became BFFs and got to hang out all the time. We don't know.

But what I do know is that she went on being Jael. The wife of Heber the Kenite. The mother of his children, the preparer of meals, the changer of diapers, the herder of sheep, the tearing down and setting up of tents. She may not have seen her outward public influence grow but in one act she helped save a nation and halt any further attacks from this enemy. You are equipped to fight battles that others can't. Never forget that. And when you do, you send reverberations in the spirit, giving glory to God. Causing others to turn to Him in worship. Allowing Jesus to be lifted up over and over again, drawing people to Him.

Release

1. What has God uniquely equipped you and only you to fight with? What tools are in your hand that have been sharpened by your faithfulness?

2. What are some things that have gotten too familiar in your household that need to be destroyed? Is this something you can get other members of your family involved in if it applies?

Milk & Honey: Overflow

He wants us.

Heart mind and soul positioned in His presence,

positioned in the flow of His heart toward us.

The us that He fully knows and fully loves.

Yet sometimes all we offer are our works or leftovers,

counterfeits that don't tell the whole story

or sometimes leave the picture blurry.

He wants us.

That's what the price was paid for.

Jesus brings us into full relationship with Him

so that out of the overflow we see things shift.

Out of the overflow we see atmospheres change.

Our works then become anointed agents of change.

Lights in darkness come from the ones

close to the Flame.

Chapter Fifteen: Encourage and Empower

The Bible is full of men and women whose small and large decisions released ripples into the culture around them. No move was wasted, and by the grace of God the ones done that didn't reflect His nature had the opportunity to be redeemed. Each person played a significant role, whether they realized it in that moment or didn't know until they stepped across the veil into eternity. If it was the same for them, it is the same for us. When we open the Word, we look into a mirror that reflects ourselves. Our ways, our tendencies, our quirks and shortcomings. But in that mirror, we should not forget to see how God used the ordinary and overly talented people, the daily and once in a lifetime happenings, to come together to work out His purpose. Every position of His people is purposeful, every season significant to the release of His kingdom and glory on the earth. Every story intended to point to His plan for humanity and ultimately give Him glory.

We cannot forget that influence is not only relegated to the well-known and well-equipped. God does powerfully glorious things with very public figures whose hearts are beautifully positioned in His presence. This is what I would personally call Macro-influence, influence that touches people on a widespread scale. Along with Macro, are the words Mezzo and Micro. These are terms used to describe different levels whether it be systems, analysis, institutions or as in the case of this part, influence. If Macro-influence is on a larger, public, and more widespread scale then Mezzo is the next level of influence. Not worse but just bringing impact to a different sphere. This level involves cities, communities, church, maybe your school or social media network. Lastly Micro-influence takes places in small circles, groups, families and with individuals. This type of influence cannot be discounted because it is this level that makes up the next and so on. And when we consider our lives in Christ, many times, the deepest and most significant moves are done in the secret, quiet and still places. Where intercession and obedience are making moves that can't be seen with the naked eye. Generational shifts happen when one person makes the decision to choose well, stand in the gap and leave the ripples and potential influence in the hands of our all-knowing and timeless God.

Because God is outside of time, He sees everything from the beginning to the end. So when we come into agreement with Him, we have the ability to pull down solutions and deliverance that not only impacts the here and now but can reach into the past or the future and shift the ground. Uprooting what was never supposed to be planted and/or plant what is needed to harvest now or in the future. That means that no matter what season you find yourself in you always have the opportunity and ability to make eternal impact. As my friend shared one day, you can shoot arrows into the future to land at the most opportune time, for the Lord to use as He sees fit. He is already there. He already knows the solution needed and when you lean into His whisper, into the things not yet known, you can shake and dismantle mountains before they have a chance to exist. Who is brave enough for that type of influence? For the influence that may not see notoriety now but is confident of a seat in heavenly places, that seeks the reward of the Lord's presence and His favor.

So, what is it that I am saying to you? Among the myriad of words and books that are already out there, among the images and posts and feeds that fill your mind's eye at every waking moment. I don't come necessarily to add to but to walk in my unique lane of release so that you can walk in yours. This piece must also be significant, this piece must also be released as you are to also release yours. Maybe the ripple will be enough to wake you from your slumber, to strip off your regret, to deliver you from a lie that is holding you captive, or to give fresh wind and vision to your dreams.

When both Deborah and Jael released their individual influence, they became unique illustrations of what the Lord had promised to the people of Israel. Remember the verse that was shared at the opening of this book. It was God's desire to deliver His people from Egypt and put them in a land flowing with Milk and Honey. This promise is not to be ignored just because it was given in the Old Testament. I firmly believe, as so many others do, that the Old Testament is a foreshadowing of the New Testament. We know Jesus himself said that He did not come to abolish the law but to fulfill it. There is beautiful symmetry in the Bible. Its so amazing to see how things relate all throughout. The promise of Milk and Honey is no different. But now, it's not about a land we are physically going to for rest, but it is a person. Through Jesus we have the promised life, rest, and abundance that the Lord foreshadowed in the Old Testament. Because of that I believe that we too can flow with Milk and Honey in our lives.

A few years ago, as I studied for a message for a large gathering of women, I spent time reading about Deborah and Jael. Their stories fascinated me because for me, Deborah was a picture of a strong, capable, God-fearing woman in public leadership. And then reading about Jael reminded me of the leadership that can take place privately in our own homes. Even though I consider both of these women as leaders they also operated as servants, letting humility and honor be a part of their characters as well. As I read in my NIV study Bible I noticed some notes down below the Biblical text that brought some amazing revelation.

> "4:22 there lay Sisera...dead. With Sisera dead the kingdom of Jabin was no longer a threat. The land "flowing with milk and honey" had been saved by

the courage and faithfulness of "Bee" (see note on v. 4) and "Mountain Goat"[1].

When I read that note I was floored by what was being revealed through the story of these two women. Instead of just seeing the awesome story of Deborah and Jael, I saw the prophetic implications of their actions. You see Deborah's name means "Bee" and Jael's name means "Mountain Goat". A bee of course produces honey and a goat produces milk. Together, Deborah and Jael were allowed to represent a part of God's plan for there to be land flowing with milk and honey. I saw this as God using two women to give another perspective to His promise. That not only would the physical land flow with life, nourishment, abundance and fertility. But that if the people operated out of the overflow of their covenant with God, they too could be used to flow with spiritual milk and honey. And in doing so would give others the opportunity to taste and see that the Lord is good. It's a promise for all of us.

Even as we focused on identity and intimacy in the stories of the woman with the issue, Jairus' daughter, Martha and Mary, we need to remember that they too released influence where they were. Their need and brokenness and questions and worship affected other people around them. I find it interesting that other people started asking if they could touch the edge of Jesus's garment as detailed in Matthew 14:36. This was after the passage detailing the encounter the woman with the issue had. It makes one wonder how much her actions to receive healing influenced how other's approached Jesus. That is the goal of our influence. Not bringing people to us but ultimately leading them to Jesus. What we ourselves release is a river of abundance flowing straight from Him. If we are positioned well, we will bring the sweetness of Jesus's presence wherever we are. We will release the spiritual provision that is needed in the places God has called us to be, in whatever season we are in, wherever that is.

Do you see Him? Coming to where you are, making a place for you where He is and setting you up to release His goodness all around you.

He is coming to bring life and activate in you the reason why you were born! He's got some daughters that need to be identified, called to Him —courageous and flowing in what He has promised! The potential for the Milk and Honey of the promised land is in you if you will choose to operate in unity as the Body of Christ. We are a sisterhood put in place to display God's glory, for His kingdom come.

Go Deeper in Influence

As you operate in kingdom mentality the world is literally at your door. Nothing can hold you back from releasing powerful lingering influence when you are not held back from Jesus. Out of the overflow of Jesus's presence is what is needed for us, our families and for those around us. How that milk and honey looks in your sphere will vary but never forget that it is needed, in whatever form the Lord calls it to take. There are so many women and men that are making beautiful moves in the kingdom. They are releasing the type of influence that all the women highlighted in this book did, in their various ways.

To find more inspiration and resources that deal specifically with areas of Influence please visit www.milkandhoneywomen.com/influence

---

Gratitude

The process of writing this book has deepened my gratitude for so many. I have never been more aware of the power of the Body of Christ in my personal life than in this season. The Lord trusts us to steward our gifts, prayers, support, finances, words, and relationships, using those as instruments of His glory. I have been a recipient of so much and not a day goes by that I don't thank God for what He has poured into my life through others.

My dear husband, my crazy viking, thank you for prioritizing obedience. For hearing clearly the call of the Lord and positioning our family to follow Him, whatever the cost. It takes a strong, brave man to walk out his life in faith and I'm so thankful that God chose me to walk this journey with you. Love you babe. To my kids, my fierce four, I'm so thankful for you and your open hearts. Even when you didn't understand change, you boldly stepped into a new country, new schools, made new friends and now speak Icelandic fluently. You put your mama to shame and you make me so proud. Love you to pieces.

To the rest of my family, thank you for your love, support and release. You make goodbyes hard and phone calls so sweet. Thanks to my Icelandic family for your love and support. It's so good to be closer to all of you. Special gratitude to my mom whose legacy is woven throughout all these pages. You were the first one, calling me out, calling me to Jesus, through your life and words. Not to mention you read through the early draft, sent me beneficial tips and typos, and told me how much you loved it. To my church family, there are no words to describe what you mean to us. Thank you for your prayers and cover, for your encouragement and financial support. The seeds we sow now are because of what you've sown into us. For the people and churches in Iceland, thank you for welcoming us with open arms and for all you have done to support our journey.

So much of this book is about sisterhood and the ways that we can encourage each other in our pursuit of Identity, Intimacy and Influence in Christ. I honor all the women who operated out of their gifts and obedience to influence my own walk. Your words and lives continue to be catalysts in my own. Thank you to all the ones who took the time to review this work and lend your support through endorsements. Thank you to those of you who positioned me for breakthrough and freedom. Thank you to those who reminded me of the permission I have to write and to dream. And I am forever grateful to those of you, some living, some now standing in the cloud of witnesses, who stir the fire in me to keep going, to never stop, never settle for less than what God has for us. Thank you sisters, thank you friends.

Lastly, Jesus, where would we be without you? Thank you for making a way for us to be close to the Father through your sacrifice. Thank you for releasing to us the Holy Spirit after your resurrection. Thank you God for calling us your own, inviting us to be with you and trusting us to be vessels of your presence. Let these words and my life always bring glory to your Name. I love you with my whole heart.

—Jenny Erlingsson

About Jenny

Jenny's goal is to be a daughter first. A sometimes feisty, strong-willed, loud-laughing, solitude seeking daughter of God through Jesus Christ. That is her core position and the role that she finds the most joy in. Out of the overflow of that, she is blessed to be the wife of an incredibly amazing and handsome Viking from Iceland and a mother to four equally cute and fierce mocha drops that keep her laughing, challenged and in prayer, all day every day!

After over twelve years of pastoral ministry working with youth and women, Jenny and her family now live in beautiful Iceland as ministry workers and community members. She and her husband desire to see God move powerfully in the nation through the transforming love of Jesus. Jenny is passionate about the Body of Christ stepping boldly into their callings, engaging in each moment and in every season so that people will know Jesus. In the in between of marriage, motherhood, and ministry, she enjoys searching for a bit of solitude, a good book, and a not too sugary snack.

For more visit www.jennyerlingsson.com

Follow @:

Instagram.com/jennyerlingsson
Facebook.com/jenny.erlingsson.author

Sign up using the code to receive the monthly Milk & Honey Women Email Magazine:

Other Books by Jenny Erlingsson

Books & Devotionals
Becoming His: Finding Your Place as a Daughter of God
Milk & Honey Study & Prayer Journal
The Cultivational Planner: A Devotional Planner for
Women
The Daddy's Girl Devotional
The Daddy's Boy Devotional

Workbooks, Journals & Planners
Dwell: Bible Study & Prayer Journal
Inspired to Write: Writing Workbook
Faith Over Fear: Simple Weekly Planner & Journal
I Will Abide: Simple Weekly Planner & Journal
Creative Clarity: Simple Weekly Planner

Encouragement & Content for Women
WWW.MILKANDHONEYWOMEN.COM

Encouragement & Services for Writers
WWW.MILKANDHONEYBOOKS.COM

Follow @:
Instagram.com/jennyerlingsson
Facebook.com/jenny.erlingsson.author

PUBLISHED
BY

MILK
&
HONEY
Books

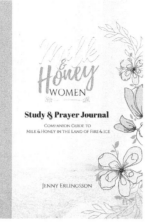

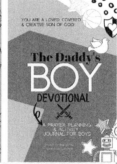

WWW.MILKANDHONEYBOOKS.COM

Endnotes

Chapter Two: Healing is on the Way

1   Robinson, Rich. *The Tallit and Tzitzit*. Jews for Jesus, January 1, 1994. https://jewsforjesus.org/publications/newsletter/newsletter-sep-1993/the-tallit-and-tzitzit/.

2   Robinson, Rich. *The Tallit and Tzitzit*. Jews for Jesus, January 1, 1994. https://jewsforjesus.org/publications/newsletter/newsletter-sep-1993/the-tallit-and-tzitzit/.

Chapter Four: Healed and Whole

1   Holism Definition, Dictionary.com, https://www.dictionary.com/browse/holism?s=t

Chapter Seven: Position over Performance

1   Platform Definition, Dictionary.com, https://www.dictionary.com/browse/platform?s=t

2   McLeod, Saul. *Erik Erikson's Stages of Psychosocial Development*. Simply Psychology, May 3, 2018. https://www.simplypsychology.org/Erik-Erikson.html

Chapter Eight: Calling out the Call

1   Erlingsson, Jenny. "Martha." *Becoming His: Finding Your Place As A Daughter of God*. Destiny Image Publishers, 2016, pg. 178

Chapter Nine: Moving with what Moves Him

1   Krulwich, Robert. "Which is Greater, The Number of Sand Grains On Earth or Stars in the Sky?", NPR, September 17, 2012. https://www.npr.org/sections/krulwich/2012/09/17/161096233/which-is-greater-the-number-of-sand-grains-on-earth-or-stars-in-the-sky?t=1581420599806.

Chapter Twelve: The Cost of Comparison

[1] *Milk.* New Christian Bible Study, https://newchristianbiblestudy.org/concept/milk

[2] Gunnars, Kris. *10 Surprising Health Benefits of Honey*, Healthline, September 5, 2018. https://www.healthline.com/nutrition/10-benefits-of-honey#section8.

Chapter Fourteen: Fighting the Familiar

[1] Erlingsson, Jenny. "Miriam." *Becoming His: Finding Your Place As A Daughter of God.* Destiny Image Publishers, 2016, pg. 59

Chapter Fifteen: Encourage and Empower

[1] Zondervan NIV Study Bible. Full ref. ed. Kenneth L. Barker, gen. ed. Grand Rapids, MI: Zondervan, 2002. Print.

Printed in Great Britain
by Amazon

85926198R10102